EXTREME ENTREPRENEURSHIP:
Inspiring Life and Business Lessons
from Entrepreneurs and Startups
around the World
(*Extreme Entrepreneurship*™ Series,
Book 1)

ADAM J. SULKOWSKI
Associate Professor of Law and Sustainability
Babson College

Cover design by Vila Design

Published by Van Rye Publishing, LLC
Ann Arbor, MI
www.vanryepublishing.com

ISBN: 978-1-7340344-4-8 (paperback)
ISBN: 978-1-7340344-5-5 (ebook)
Library of Congress Control Number: 2021941398

Praise for *Extreme Entrepreneurship*

"For *Extreme Entrepreneurship*, **Adam Sulkowski traveled to 120 countries (!), gathering the fascinating stories of business creators** from literally around the world. As you read the 1st person accounts of people making change happen in their communities—from a Pakistani bookstore owner to Malagasy women incubating food businesses around solar mini-grids—**you will be both educated and inspired.**"

> —P. W. Singer, *New York Times* best-selling author and Strategist at New America

*"**READ THIS!**"*

> —Alex Mashinsky, serial entrepreneur (20+ successful ventures), holder of 50+ patents (including VOIP), founded and leads Celsius Network (a financial platform with $13B+ in assets under management)

"This book is **a compelling set of stories about how entrepreneurs are starting businesses that change people's lives all around the world.** It renews my faith in seeing business as a force for good."

> —R. Edward Freeman, Professor of Business Administration, Darden School of Business, University of Virginia

"**Adam Sulkowski tells lively, big-hearted, and often surprising stories that anyone can read and relate to**—as an entrepreneur, parent, activist, reader, traveler, or seeker. **They tap into**

universal dimensions of the human spirit: resilience, courage, humility, curiosity, and imagination. Read and enjoy!"
—Anne-Marie Slaughter, CEO, New America

"**As a start-up founder, awesome to see practical tips**— including from fellow female founders at the frontlines of positive change—collected from super-tough environments."
—Courtney Boyd Myers, Co-Founder and CEO, Akua

"This is **a combination travelogue and business 'how to' book that establishes Adam Sulkowski as the Anthony Bourdain of entrepreneurship.** Sulkowski shares fascinating stories about entrepreneurs in parts unknown who face daunting challenges in starting their businesses. One of my favorites is the chapter on a team of women who are determined to bring solar power to villages in Madagascar."
—George Siedel, Ross School of Business, University of Michigan

"**Awesome tips for life, work, and travel.**"
—Michael Blakey, Managing Partner at Cocoon Capital Partners Pte Ltd

"**110%, I recommend this for entrepreneurs and travelers (actual, aspiring, or spectators).** You'll laugh, possibly cry, and be inspired as you get to know how these real-life heroes are doing nearly impossible things—in places most of us barely know or understand, from East Timor to Madagascar to Suriname. **You won't regret the time invested in enjoying these stories.**"
—Jason Cipriano, serial entrepreneur, executive at MassMutual, formerly State Street, 1st Lt., US Navy

"**Finally, a 'truth on the ground' approach to wisdom on entrepreneurship.**"

—Elizabeth Kim, Strategic Initiatives Specialist, Babson College

"A must-read. This book is not *just* for entrepreneurs—there's wisdom here for everyone. Each story in this book—collected from an astounding variety of environments—provides lessons on how to succeed when many factors align against you. This is an invaluable fresh twist on the kinds of research and teaching that have kept Babson the #1 rated school for entrepreneurs of all kinds for decades. **The themes and lessons of this book are both timely and timeless."**

—Leonard A. Schlesinger, Baker Foundation Professor and Chair of Practice Faculty, Harvard Business School

"Gripping and compelling stories of people and their unique journeys, challenges, and approaches to questions of strategy and sustainability."

—Sandra Waddock, Galligan Chair of Strategy, Boston College

"*Extreme Entrepreneurship* is like three books in one: travelogue, entrepreneurship case study collection, and distillation of tips on how to navigate through life. Great to see underrepresented voices elevated as a source of wisdom. And great to see so many stories related to Sustainable Development Goals (SDGs). The fact over half of the stories are those of female founders is a bonus."

—Cheryl Y. Kiser, Executive Director, Lewis Institute for Social Innovation, Babson College

"A must-read. Adam shines a light on the values that are driving these diverse protagonists—and weaves their stories into a tapestry rich with actionable lessons, universal observations on the human spirit at its best, and tips anyone can use."

—Mary C. Gentile, PhD, Professor of Practice, Darden School of Business, University of Virginia, author of *Giving Voice to Values: How to Speak Your Mind When You Know What's Right*

"**Exciting!** A strong achievement. The book subject is important. It shows entrepreneurial activity can thrive in almost any environment. **Bodes to be influential.**"

—Robert C. Bird, Professor of Business Law and Eversource Energy Chair in Business Ethics at the University of Connecticut, President, Academy of Legal Studies in Business

"**Be prepared to be moved** by all of these characters: from Liliana in Peru (helping kids that previously were kept in cages to become independent, productive, and happy) to John in Guatemala (going from homeless, to smuggling in a priest's attire, to becoming an export baron with a heart). Partly a travel memoir, partly a collection of interviews and stories brimming with wisdom on business and life, this is **a fantastic voyage to meet inspiring heroes in unfamiliar places with universal lessons.**"

—Dariusz Jemielniak, serial entrepreneur, Professor of Organizational Studies at Kozminski University, Faculty Associate at the Berkman Center at Harvard University

"**Fascinating, informed, and informative!**"

—Manoj Narender Madnani, Founder and CEO, The DSA Group

"**A book full of leadership lessons in sustainability!** Entrepreneurship in food systems and renewable energy is essential as the world seeks innovative business solutions in the face of global climate change. **From Colombia to Madagascar, the inspiring stories in this book underscore the possibility of entrepreneurial leadership applied in the global context.** The stories include great details without losing sight of the big picture."

—Rockford "Rocky" Weitz, serial entrepreneur (8 ventures), Professor of Practice and Director of the Fletcher Maritime Studies Program at Tufts University

"Tomorrow's disruptive innovations often evolve first on the edges of today's systems. Over time, the more successful ones fold into the core of our societies and economies. They become the new normal. As these innovations accumulate, the prevailing paradigm begins to shift. And then, before we know it, reality isn't what it used to be. **Adam Sulkowski's *Extreme Entrepreneurship* takes us to the edge of the known**, into worlds darkened by poaching, civil war, and even genocide, bringing extraordinary change agents into the spotlight. **Unsettling—in a positive way—and deeply informative.**"

—John Elkington, serial entrepreneur, Chief Pollinator at Volans Ventures, and author of 20 books, most recently *Green Swans: The Coming Boom in Regenerative Capitalism* (Fast Company Press)

"Having worked closely with the author, this collection of stories is what we've come to expect: making space for **an array of gifted people at the fringes of mainstream economic opportunity to tell their amazing stories.**"

—Sadie Burton-Goss, Chief Diversity and Inclusion Officer, Babson College

"It was fun to cooperate in telling our stories! **Please enjoy.**"

—Lydia Wanjiku Kibandi, CEO, Lensational, and
—Lieutenant Colonel Faye Cuevas, US Air Force

Contents

Preface

Why Go to 120 Countries? Why Collect Stories of Startups?

I
T WAS 2005. I felt I'd won the lottery. I had received a job offer for a full-time job teaching law at a business school. After being unemployed for a few dark months that felt like years, I literally went from down-and-out to being on track to security in a dream job. I would be paid to help students interested in commerce learn about law for eight months of the year. The other four, I'd be free (and expected) to write. And I could do that writing anywhere.

Yet I felt like a charlatan—a phony. Not because I hadn't spent time practicing law or running a business. But because I'd been reading books about life in "the Global South"—as we euphemistically started calling poor countries—and how the world was much more connected than the 4 percent of us in the US imagined. Plus, I'd been reading about sustainability and the fragility of both environmental and economic systems.

I was about to teach eighteen- to twenty-two-year-olds about business. Eventually, MBAs as well. And yet I'd never set foot on most continents. I'd never been to a factory in China, a war zone, or a bazaar in the Middle East or transacted with someone in the ocean of humanity in a city of more than 15 million people like Mumbai. I'd never seen rainforest stewardship by Indigenous peoples or by intact communities founded by escaped slaves or encountered a jaguar mother and cub deep in the Amazon. Nor had I met someone fine with cutting all these jungles down, so long as he got his share of the cash. I'd never imagined how much I'd see malnutrition resulting from modern neocolonial trade patterns replacing locally-sourced food. I'd never eaten in a slum anywhere, walked through a refugee camp's gates, or fallen asleep knowing that a Muslim call to prayer would wake me up.

In short, I felt like a charlatan because I was about to explain aspects of business in the world, but I'd lived in the realities that less than 10 percent of us call home. I had zero firsthand experience in the reality that more than 90 percent of people call home. And it's now become cliché to observe, but we're all connected through business and the functioning and fate of the natural environment. If I was going to teach law to business students, I thought I should see and know more about the world out there. So, I looked up old friends, spent the lion's share of the last of my savings on plane tickets, and hopped onto a flight to Africa and later that year to Asia. That was the start.

Having now visited 120 countries—and through a mix of gobsmackingly unlikely luck and serendipity, the suggestions and help of others, and sometimes intentional searching, and despite more missteps than I'd like to admit—I've met and collected stories of people who've started solving problems by creating organizations in some seemingly impossible conditions. Based on these stories, it turns out that some challenges are universal. Other stories fascinate because they're specific to a place, time, or person. I've shared some of these stories in classrooms and online with hundreds of students over the years. We practice spotting problems and opportunities, applying theory to practice, and trying to answer: "what will we do when we find ourselves in a similar situation?"

Here, finally, in this book is a collection of some of my students' favorite stories from entrepreneurs I have met during my travels. The reaction of my students is one reason I know that these stories stir emotions and curiosity. At times, the contexts of these stories may sadden. In other moments, a vignette may make you laugh. The most common comment I've read in anonymous student surveys is that these stories *inspire*.

Some of the stories about entrepreneurs and startups contained in this book I've told before, in a longer, more academic format. When I've shared them, some have won awards from organizations dedicated to legal studies and to entrepreneurship. This also suggests something may be learned from these stories. But in contrast to academic contexts, the stories published here—some of them for the first time—have a greater focus on the people involved and a greater emphasis on each story's context and the aspects that are entertaining, inspiring, and thought-provoking.

Having published over fifty times in scholarly research journals and conference proceedings, it is wonderful to finally tell stories without using the fancy jargon that is the norm for academic writing (plus, in the case of legal writing, hundreds of footnotes referencing supporting sources of information). I also have never shared this much detail about the stories before. If there is an entertaining or enlightening backstory—the why and how—of how I came to meet someone, then I've included it. You, the reader, could find lessons or inspiration in some of these individual backstories. If you ask me, some examples of these possible takeaways are:

- action is sometimes better than exhaustive planning;
- it pays to show up, ask questions, and ask for help in what you're trying to achieve;

- it's sometimes okay to have a tendency to say "yes" to life's random opportunities; and
- maybe above all, to stay curious.

You may, however, draw other lessons, make your own observations, and come to your own conclusions. Additionally—or instead—you might read some of my confessions about how I came to meet the people featured in this book and conclude that I'm a bit eccentric in how I spend time on my semester breaks. Either way, I've kept the spotlight on the main characters and their stories, and I've included a selection of stories that I know to be "audience favorites," varied in terms of context and similar but different.

I am keenly aware the world is filled with thousands more stories like the ones in this book. I did *not* attempt, with this collection, to generate a portfolio that is representative of the world nor that is proportionate to the scale and difficulty of problems that countries and the world collectively face. I'm hoping the stories in this book are a first collection. And maybe it will inspire more stories like these.

Thanks to all the people described in this book for sharing their stories and entrusting me to tell them. My thanks also to students and colleagues who provided feedback and encouragement. And thanks to you, the reader, for reading these stories. I hope you're entertained and inspired and maybe even find something useful.

Introduction

Intended Use for This Book

Why I wrote this book

This book was written to:

- entertain by sharing some good stories;
- inspire with examples of people succeeding in difficult circumstances;
- introduce relatable problems from unfamiliar places; and
- raise awareness of challenges (and great ideas for overcoming them).

The stories in this book were written with the following readers in mind:

- entrepreneurs (of all kinds—plus those who aspire to be entrepreneurs or who just enjoy spectating);
- travel addicts (those who are traveling, going to travel, planning to travel, or are enjoying travel vicariously); and
- last but not least, the just plain curious (learners of any age and in any context).

Earlier drafts of these stories have been:

- shared with people who have started companies;
- reviewed by colleagues who teach in business schools; and

- used with students as issue-spotting exercises in business school courses.

My hopes for readers of this book

For the aspiring entrepreneur or the entrepreneurial leader of any organization:

From those entrepreneurs interviewed and described in this book, I hope you find inspiration and useful ideas for how to see, hear, think, plan, and act.

For the aspiring traveler, or you on the road, or you who misses traveling:

Similarly, we (those entrepreneurs profiled in each chapter and I) hope you find inspiration and actionable ideas, even if you're limited in how far you can travel and are presently enjoying vicarious voyages.

For students (whether in school or reading this as an autodidactic):

I hope you find the stories in this book entertaining and useful for several things:

- issue-spotting, meaning defining exactly what is a problem;
- practice in applying abstract concepts and imagining options for action; and
- learning about the contexts of parts of the world that might be unfamiliar to you.

Format of this book

The chapter formats will vary slightly. My top priority was to convey the words and reflections of the people at the center of each startup story. Therefore, some chapters almost exclusively consist of reordered and repackaged highlights of interviews. A second priority was to convey context and the story of how I met these people, inasmuch as those stories may be interesting or valuable as well. Regardless of the format, each chapter ends with an enumerated list of takeaways that you, the reader, can apply to your business or personal life.

Here's hoping you find something valuable and interesting in the stories in this book. And I wish you good luck in your adventures. If you have questions or know of similar stories that you think I should consider for a follow-up book, please do not hesitate to contact me directly—my contact information appears in the About the Author section toward the back of this book. In addition, to read or hear my most recent stories and conversations with people like the ones in this book, please visit: www.extreme-entrepreneurship.com.

Chapter Summaries
Each Story in a Nutshell

1. Peru: A Pioneering School for the Differently-Abled Built during a War Faces COVID-19

As punishment for asking questions, a student is banished to work with outcasts: kids with cerebral palsy, Down syndrome, and autism. She finds her life calling: to co-teach (with their families) these kids to be independent, productive, and happy. She built her school with volunteers using discarded wood during a civil war from 1980–1992, sometimes carrying a white flag to avoid being shot. Forty years later, her work has touched 15,000 families in seven countries. The drop in donations due to the COVID-19 pandemic, ongoing at the time of this writing, has presented their greatest challenge so far, even though their work in homeschooling support and distance learning should be more valued now than ever.

2. Pakistan: She Persisted Selling Books at The Last Word

Despite extremist violence and betrayal by unscrupulous businessmen, a community comes together to support Aysha and her business selling Western and secular books in Pakistan.

3. Timor-Leste: Pride in Local Food and Hunger for Information after a Genocide

In the wake of genocide, in a smoldering city with not a single working computer left, local journalists and an Australian with access to discarded equipment start a newspaper. Now, a local chef is reviving pride in local food after globalization leads to malnutrition.

4. Guatemala: Broke to Smuggler to Legal Exporter of Ilegal Mezcal

The path to sharing wealth with local artisans involves navigating a corrupt and dangerous border.

5. Madagascar: Empowering Local Economies in Villages with Solar Mini-Grid 3.0

By building relationships, a team of women executes a plan to bring solar power into villages to nurture small businesses and encourage the re-localized production of nutrient-rich food.

6. Colombia: Resurrecting Rainforest during a Civil War

Both sides of a civil war spared a decades-old reforestation community that continues inventing novel products and solutions.

7. Kenya: A Counter-Terrorism Officer Targets Poachers by Listening to Locals

An intelligence officer (and single mother of three) working with US Special Forces in combat zones starts noticing correlations in early warning indicators ahead of terrorist and poaching incidents. She gets "left of boom" and starts advocating for women's entrepreneurship as a key to winning cooperation with local communities in both contexts.

8. Cuba: From One Dollar per Day to Top-Rated Place to Stay

Though capitalism is officially illegal, a former tailor starts and grows a top-rated hostel.

9. United States: Cooking-Up a Revival in a Former Mill Town

Two friends lead an economic renaissance along an economically stagnant main street of a small town.

10. Suriname: Preserving the Maroon Culture and Rainforest in a Pandemic

For centuries, descendants of escaped slaves have farmed sustainably in the jungles of Suriname, preserving a unique culture. Illegal mining increasingly devastates these rainforests.

11. Outer Space and Inner Space: Astrophysicist to Heart Hacker and MindMics

An astrophysicist develops a platform for using earbuds to gather precise medical data.

Chapter 1

Peru: A Pioneering School for the Differently-Abled Built during a War Faces COVID-19

TO AVOID BEING SHOT, Dr. Liliana Mayo carried a white flag when crossing parts of Lima to pick up volunteers for her pioneering school for the differently-abled, as she insists on calling her students. Dr. Mayo's innovative experiments in education as a psychology student starting in 1979 coincided with the increased activity of a local terrorist movement. Deadly violence, plus power and water outages, would become part of the second longest-running civil war in recent Latin American history, lasting from 1980 until 1992. This was the context in which Mayo developed her unique way of, as she stated it, "providing a first-world service in third world poverty with fourth world compensation." Actually, Dr. Mayo achieved something that had not been done before, even in the most developed countries in the world: her school has arguably been *better* than a first-world service.

The following sections of this chapter are excerpts from my interviews with Dr. Mayo and describe the incredible true story of a student sent—as punishment—to work with children who were outcasts. In doing so, Dr. Mayo found her life's mission in helping them become independent, productive, and happy. She built a school with no resources during a civil war, improved the lives of 15,000 families across seven countries, and is now facing the most difficult challenge of her life: run on donations, Centro Ann Sullivan Peru (CASP) is, at the time of this writing, in dire financial straits due to the COVID-19 pandemic.

1.1. Dr. Liliana Mayo with a former student of her school, Centro Ann Sullivan Peru (CASP), named Patty, in Lima, Peru. (Image courtesy of Dr. Liliana Mayo.)

From punishment to finding her life's mission

As a psychology student, Dr. Mayo had made the fateful error of asking questions that irritated one of her professors. Her temporary punishment-by-banishment—exile, to work among children with special needs—turned out to be where she realized her life's mission. On the way to work, in poorer neighborhoods, Dr. Mayo saw that children with autism, cerebral palsy, and Down syndrome were sometimes kept naked and tied up or in cages on rooftops like maltreated animals. Upon learning that a child was neurologically atypical, many men would abandon their wives and families. Dr. Mayo was sure there was a better way to raise and educate these children.

How to even begin the impossible, with nothing? How did she find resources?

Dr. Mayo credits her parents with letting her use the garage of their home to try a different approach to teaching differently-abled children. In so crediting them, she attests to the value of sharing one's crazy ambitions with others. As another example of this value, Dr. Mayo recalls sharing her dream and her needs early on with someone and soon receiving a donation of eight chairs for her first students to sit upon.

That first benefactor, who donated the chairs, had been "looking for a mission" and had informed others—including her husband, a local businessperson—of Dr. Mayo's needs. He donated scrap wood—the remnants of boxes used for transporting windows from a factory—as the first building material. Off-duty police agreed to provide the first carpentry services, with so many showing up at Dr. Mayo's home that "neighbors thought there must be drug trafficking going on," she recalls.

Dr. Mayo reflected: "You never know what will happen when

you are ready and apply learning and tell people what you need. . . . When we most need it, a miracle arrives." This theme consistently emerges in other stories in this book: that people—including acquaintances and strangers—can be surprisingly encouraging and critically helpful when they learn of a chance to help someone realize a crazy—yet positive and constructive—dream. Forty years later, CASP helps hundreds of students around Peru and the world every year to become, in the words of its slogan, "independent, productive, and happy" and has inspired similar centers in several countries.

Dr. Mayo's focus: persons with different abilities

Dr. Mayo insists on calling her students "persons with different abilities" to highlight two things. First, that they are people—not a label. Second, that we have to concentrate more on their abilities, not their limitations. She strongly believed that her students could be independent, productive, and happy if she (and now, her instructors) work as a team with her students' families. Dr. Mayo and her team call this "the power of two." And they have consistently demonstrated the effectiveness of this approach.

"I can't die yet . . ."

Dr. Mayo recalls telling herself, in 1980, as she crossed violence-torn Lima, "You can't die until you teach the children." The violence of the civil war would continue from 1980–1992. Through the pandemic of 2020–2021, which has been especially destructive in Peru, she said she did not waiver in her resolve. "I can't die until every person with different abilities in my country has the opportunity—them and their families—to receive an education."

In developing her expertise, mostly acquired through real-world experimentation, Dr. Mayo showed that neurologically-atypical children can be taught to be independent, productive, and happy. More than one hundred students who received their education at CASP are now working adults contributing to more than forty businesses in the private and public sectors. They have proven that they can perform excellently in different jobs. For example, they excel as banking professionals due to their long attention spans, quantitative abilities, and scrupulousness, among other traits. However, as described later, Dr. Mayo's journey was far from smooth and safe, and it contains several generalizable lessons for anyone.

What were the key factors to CASP's success (that could help in any situation)?

Dr. Mayo says that passion and having a team are the two factors that led to CASP's success.

Where did Dr. Mayo's passion come from, and why aren't there more people like her?

I had previously guessed Dr. Mayo's answer might be that a lot of us behave monstrously because we are rewarded for—and see the idolization of—the acquisition of wealth and fame. Instead, she attributed her mindset, values, and readiness to act to her parents. She credited her parents for giving her inspiration and values and for serving as role models: "My parents were pharmacists—I saw them providing a service in poor neighborhoods, and my mom told me all about MLK [the lesson being, to paraphrase Martin Luther King Jr., 'to be persistent, to follow the impossible dream'] . . . and JFK [the lesson being, to paraphrase John F. Kennedy, 'to ask what you can do for others, not what others can do for you'] . . . and Mohandas Gandhi [the lesson being, to paraphrase Gandhi, 'to be the change you wish to see in the world']."

What about the other factor: how did Dr. Mayo find her team?

In response to this question, Dr. Mayo described telling people about the dream she had for who would work at the school. She looked for two things: a good heart and open-mindedness. Five people who joined her in the early days of her school are still with her on her current team of eighty. This echoes a theme found in other stories in this book: skills can be taught, and so instead it may sometimes be equally or more important to screen and hire for character, disposition, and other "hard-wired" (or difficult-to-acquire) traits than to hire based on skills. Again, Dr. Mayo cites her parents for creating the conditions that taught her what to look for: she was made to do her chores, was made to see obstacles as opportunities, was taught how to be happy, and was taught that "you only have what you give."

The early years and a new approach: respect and listening

Dr. Mayo said that a critical factor in her first successes was listening to her students. She is convinced that they felt and understood what was conveyed nonverbally: most critically, that she respected them as people. One of her first eight students was a girl named Patty (pictured at the start of this chapter, in a black-and-white childhood photograph, and in a more recent photograph at the end of this section). Mayo recalls: "I have never seen tantrums as horrible as hers. She would slap her own face. She could destroy a room. Some thought she needed an exorcism. But she was my teacher."

The books on differently-abled persons said Patty would learn slowly, if at all. Mayo found otherwise. "Once we began to work with her and teach her other ways to ask for what she wants, she began to change. She was my inspiration. She's the one who gave me hope that these kids could learn. If she could learn so fast, then we were using a correct approach." By 1981, there were fifty students.

1.2. Dr. Liliana Mayo with a former student of her school, Centro Ann Sullivan Peru (CASP), named Patty, in Lima, Peru. (Image courtesy of Dr. Liliana Mayo.)

Teaching kindness and giving

From the beginning, CASP taught students to give back, including to their parents—to "pay for light and water and to take their parents to dinner, to take care of them when they are sick or in cases of emergencies. And kindness—to say 'hi' and 'thank you.'" Also, Dr. Mayo emphasizes her belief that "adversity is how you grow faster."

The devastating impact of COVID-19

Dr. Mayo emphasizes that she still believes, especially in this time of COVID-19, that there are both crises and opportunities. Specifically, Peru has suffered unusually-high fatality rates and a devastating blow to an economy in which annual income averaged $500—before the shutdown of economic activity—as well as suffering a decline in charitable donations. CASP has had to furlough employees and cut down on some in-person activities.

CASP: ahead of its time in assisting with distance learning and homeschooling

CASP was an early pioneer in distance learning and supporting homeschooling. As previously mentioned, from the beginning, the essential foundation of Dr. Mayo's approach was the "power of two." Namely, training families to be essential partners in co-teaching their children. Even as there is a dire shortfall in fundraising, there is a greater need than ever before for this core competency.

What about changing CASP's model, to not rely on donations?

Ironically, the COVID-19 pandemic has hurt CASP financially, even as its expertise in distance learning and support for families teaching their children at home is revealed to be more valuable than ever. I asked Dr. Mayo if there's any chance of adopting another financial model—one more like a business, where the employers of CASP alumni (who enjoy the operational and reputational benefits of hiring them) pay for their tuition. "No, we've asked," replied Dr. Mayo. "They don't seem to be ready, and this doesn't seem to be the right time for something like that."

Dr. Mayo has a point: the COVID-19 financial shortfall is *now*. Both CASP and the companies are short on cash. Companies short on cash don't feel they have the extra money on hand for what would be, at present, a donation. And even if they agreed to pay for the education of a potential future hire over time, this would not address the need for money CASP has today.

Another potential adaptation would be for CASP to expand its training and distance learning practices to reach richer regions of the world and then charge more for its services there. This would effectively subsidize CASP programs in less-wealthy regions. Apparently, this is a possibility.

Is it true that some males do not stay involved with their children?

"In Peru," Dr. Mayo explained, "fathers of children diagnosed with autism or other disabilities would sometimes abandon their families. This has changed since the 1970s. It does not happen as often." Still, Dr. Mayo does teach mothers entrepreneurship—helping them to succeed in making income with their own economic activity. Dr. Mayo checked after our conversation and confirmed that thirty mothers in CASP's network are now abandoned. Dr. Mayo calls them "courageous." Both mothers and fathers are also trained to be "life" coaches, and Dr. Mayo employs them. She also helps them to get hired elsewhere or to sell goods as street merchants, making their own income.

Mentors and "the children are my teachers now"

Dr. Mayo described Dr. Judy LeBlanc from the University of Kansas and their thirty-eight years of cooperation as key to CASP's success, and also Dr. Steve Schroeder. Dr. Mayo said they both saved her from a few mistakes, such as accepting a government job. Dr. Mayo hastened to add: "Children are my teachers, and my son Alonso is another mentor now."

Why does Dr. Mayo believe her innovative approach was developed in Peru, not in Europe or the US?

"Poverty pushes us to make our students independent," Dr. Mayo pointed out. There is "no help from the government to families that have children with different abilities. . . . So, this is why we teach the families to be partners in the education of their child and to work in a team with the professionals."

What was your toughest challenge?

I expected that Dr. Mayo would say her toughest challenge was turning away a child or family—deciding that someone could not be helped. "No," she answered, "we have never turned anyone away." Dr. Mayo elaborated that "ANY child can be helped if the family is willing to help." She clarified: "We don't do miracles. We treat them like a human. We set high expectations. We emphasize the 'power of two'—meaning that the parents must be actively engaged as our partners."

The reader will likely be surprised by what Dr. Mayo identified as the toughest challenge she remembers—prior to the pandemic of 2020, that is. She said it was "flattening the hierarchy of the organization more than twenty to twenty-five years ago." This echoes what other entrepreneurs articulate as being difficult: eventually, growing a business and expanding its impacts requires the trade-off of sharing and delegating control and decisions.

Dr. Mayo echoed precisely that point, saying: "It means delegating, entrusting, giving up a degree of ownership and control—it's tough to do, you have to work on your own ego—it's not 'my event' anymore." Her mentors advised the flattening of the organization and sharing of responsibilities, she recalls, "so as to improve teamwork and motivation." She noted that "There are now five people ready to take my position—there are shared decisions and attention. That is because we let others feel they could make a decision." This is good because Dr. Mayo said she is in "a process of detachment" and now is "looking for ways to make it [CASP] truly self-sustainable financially."

Any disappointments?

Dr. Mayo recalls that she cried when she saw "a previous student of ours who was overweight and begging in the street—he had such potential when I saw him the first time when he was six years old. If only his family had committed to working with him. What wasted potential, . . . what he could have been. This is why it is so important to work with the families in a team."

Anything more, after forty years, that you have learned that you want to communicate about the neurologically atypical?

"They understand more than we know. Sometimes I work with

students, and I don't know their language, but they know how I talk to them and from all my nonverbal behavior that I believe in what they can do. We always are using the phrase 'I believe in you, . . . YOU CAN.'"

Any advice that you have for others, based on your experience, which they can use in their own efforts?

"The reason we succeed is that we believe that children with different abilities can be independent, productive, and happy if we work in a team with the families. We have demonstrated this for forty years. We focus on their abilities: on what they CAN do. We treat them as they want to be treated."

Dr. Mayo elaborated: "Again, it is very important we work in a team with the families. This is why we have the School of Families at CASP, where we trained more than 400 families every fifteen days to be the best parent-teachers for their child. If we didn't work with the families, we would never have obtained the success we're having with our students. Parents traveled with their children with different abilities to other provinces in Peru to make the multiplicative effect of teaching other parents."

1.3. Dr. Liliana Mayo with a student at her school, Centro Ann Sullivan Peru (CASP), in Lima, Peru. (Image courtesy of Dr. Liliana Mayo.)

Takeaway lessons that could help you in other situations in life and business

(1) A setback—or even a "punishment"—could lead to something positive, possibly even discovering one's mission in life and founding a pioneering organization.

(2) Do not underestimate people—even those who are written-off or differently-abled. By listening and showing respect, you may unlock undiscovered potential.

(3) Telling people about your crazy but constructive ambitions can result in a surprising amount of support.

(4) Key factors to success in this story include passionately believing in a cause and other people, growing a team, and a service-oriented and positive mindset.

(5) Trial and error, in reality, can sometimes lead to breakthroughs in areas where theories (or plans based on theories) have to date failed to provide a clear path toward solutions.

(6) A lack of resources can sometimes force experimentation, methods, discoveries, and results that are better than a context with an abundance of resources.

(7) Focus on what can be done rather than on limitations.

(8) Magnifying your impact and leaving a sustainable legacy requires, at some point, delegating authority and trusting others.

(9) Share and be proud of what you do but remain teachable and open to input.

Chapter 2

Pakistan: She Persisted Selling Books at The Last Word

PAKISTAN: KNOWN TO Americans as, among other things, Osama bin Laden's last hideout. I visited in 2010 with a colleague keen on meeting the Kalash, a unique religious and ethnic minority in the Hindu Kush mountain range along the Afghan border. Our trek to visit the Kalash began in Lahore, the home of attorney, environmental activist, and my friend Ahmad "Rafay" Alam, whose wife, Aysha Raja, opened the bookstore The Last Word (www.thelastwordbks.com) in Lahore in 2007.

2.1. The Shahi Masjid mosque, in Chitral, Pakistan, near the Kalasha Valleys. (Image by Adam J. Sulkowski.)

Context

Lahore is Pakistan's second-largest city—a bustling and historic metropolis of over 11 million people and a center of culture and education. Still, from the confiscation of alcohol upon arrival to the attire of some people to the multiple, simultaneous calls to prayer echoing five times per day, there is little doubt in the mind of a visitor that one is in an Islamic republic. This sense is reinforced if one enters Pakistan from India at an entry point near Lahore and witnesses the passionate displays of national pride at the daily closing of the Wagah border crossing.

The several years preceding our visit in 2010 were a less than safe and stable time. Parts of the country had been under militant control, and terror attacks, including in Islamabad and Lahore, had claimed thousands of lives. In 2009 alone, over 2,500 attacks resulted in over 3,000 deaths in Pakistan. In fairness, the homicide rate can be higher in the US than in Pakistan in a typical year, and yet, Pakistanis will admit that this was a generally subpar era in their country. During our visit in 2010, a political party aligned with religious militants held a very open and public political march in Lahore's center. Given this context, even in cosmopolitan and progressive Lahore, owning and holding events in a bookstore with secular and progressive literature, including foreign titles from the West, seemed like a risky activity, especially for a new mother.

Aysha decides she wants The Last Word

When I asked Aysha what motivated her to open a bookstore, she explained, "I couldn't find any books I wanted to read and resented having to leave town to stock up on books." This frustration, coupled with the fact that she was a new mother and her multinational employer was unwilling to offer her a flexible schedule or workplace childcare facilities, helped convince Aysha that the time was right for her to satisfy her own needs, and those of others in the community, for everything that a bookstore can offer a community.

Although she had enough of her own funds to get started and could avoid taking loans, Aysha recalls that there were "a lot of people in the book business deterring me from joining," and some went so far as to describe her idea as a "doomed enterprise." While not explicit, some of the discouragement and the adversity that Aysha encountered could well have been rooted in bias against her as a woman entrepreneur.

2.2. Aysha Raja at the bookstore she founded and owns, The Last Word, in Lahore, Pakistan. (Image by Javaria Waseem.)

What was it like when you were starting?

Aysha recalls a period of time in her first location during which she was threatened and bullied by "a landlord who had his own business on the same premises which didn't do too well." Aysha described that "at one point I was physically assaulted before I was able to get a restraining order of sorts. He still never quite left me alone until my lease was up."

Why didn't a bookstore with Western titles provoke a reaction from militant extremists?

The answer lies partly in the means through which Aysha attracted new clientele. New customers learned about The Last Word through word of mouth. When I asked if she was ever concerned about a risk of attracting a protest or attack, Aysha replied: "At one point, when I did an event on blasphemy, yes." But overall, because of its reliance on word-of-mouth promotion, the bookstore "didn't attract dangerous types."

2.3. People attending an event at Aysha Raja's bookstore, The Last Word, in Lahore, Pakistan. (Image by Javaria Waseem.)

A surprising insight (for outsiders, at least): some fundamentalists turned out to be fans

The most surprising insight about society in Lahore emerged when we continued discussing the topic of fear in a context in which ideological disagreements can turn violent. Aysha explained: "As for fundamentalists, I have many customers who appear conservative. They wear beards and shalwar kurta, but they're never irked by me. Also, there are full-veil women who have been very appreciative of our efforts."

I asked, do some very religious people in Pakistan appreciate a bookstore with literature (and therefore ideas) that may be secular or progressive and clearly not associated with Islam? "Yeah, I have one bearded and capped fellow who regularly brings his daughter to our story time. Loves it," Aysha said, adding that "by and large the community is very appreciative and protective of the business. For some, it's a source of pride for the city."

2.4. A speaker at an event at Aysha Raja's bookstore, The Last Word, in Lahore, Pakistan. (Image by Javaria Waseem.)

What was Aysha's toughest obstacle, and how did she overcome it?

As it turns out, Aysha's toughest hurdle was not related to protests by fundamentalists or attacks by militants but to fairly generic dishonesty. And she overcame this hurdle thanks to the loyalty and support of the community described immediately above. As Aysha explained:

> Exactly a year ago, I was evicted from my second premises. As luck would have it, my new landlord (actually a middle-man, since he was subletting to me) absconded without paying the landowner. The entire community went out of their way to buy books from my house. The community made sure I had enough for security. Some who knew the landowner, who resided in Karachi, gave references and a guarantee that we were good people who were just caught in the middle of a horrible fraud. We managed to re-enter a contract with the building owner in Karachi (who is also a woman) and have been happily conducting business.

There are a few takeaway lessons from the experience Aysha relates. One would be that, even with a contract in place, sometimes people break their word. As illustrated in other stories in this book, when the rule of law or honesty or an enforceable agreement are absent, it seems that reputation and—most importantly— relationships are key to the ability to continue functioning.

What was your toughest decision?

A crisis like the one described above can sometimes clarify what must be done, while tough decision points may arise when there is a lack of a clear emergency. As Aysha described: "The Last

Word has been around for more than ten years, and the toughest decision for me was three years ago when I closed down the 'concessions.' Concessions were more like wall displays [we had up] at other places of business and for value addition. So, I didn't pay rent. I closed them to open what I call the 'flagship' store, which is the only location [that I have now]."

For Aysha, moving back to a single-store model has meant "putting in more hours, and the risk was greater now." Aysha explained that "raising the stakes has been the toughest decision I made, but what made the risk worth it was that I had established a loyal clientele and reputation, so word of mouth spread fast."

What lessons would you pass on to your daughter (or any businessperson)?

Aysha's wisdom for aspiring entrepreneurs is to preserve their personal lives away from work: "It is hard, but try to put some space between yourself and your business. With such extreme highs and lows, it really messes with your mental health and sense of self-worth." Specifically, Aysha takes the following steps: "I no longer go into work every day but have an office at home which is a more tranquil space. All this is as an effort to turn down some of the pressure that can take a toll on your daily life and relationships." She quickly added: "I do, however, read to kids on a weekly basis, and I would not miss that for the world."

Postscript

I mentioned at the start of this chapter that my time in Lahore was part of a longer trip, the purpose of which was to visit the Kalash. Our hosts believed that my traveling companion (a history professor specializing in events in the so-called War on Terror, Brian Glyn Williams) and I were the first Americans to traverse what had very recently been Taliban-held territory, from 2007–2009. We stayed in Rumbur—one of the three valleys where a few thousand Kalash live traditional lives. The Kalash had no advance notice that we, the only visitors, would be arriving. Therfore, we are quite sure that what we experienced was not an orchestrated charade to create photo opportunities for visitors.

Based on everything we saw, the Kalash valleys truly are a pocket of preserved culture and lifestyles. The valley appeared unpolluted and idyllic, to such extent that fruit can be gathered from under trees and eaten. Our gracious hosts showed us their religious sites and decided to fête the occasion with wine of their own making and music performed on improvised instruments. Our only regret was not budgeting more time to stay and learn about this unique culture in the mountains leading up to the Himalayan range.

Takeaway lessons that could help you in other situations in life and business

(1) "Scratching your own itch"—in other words, identifying a way to satisfy your own needs—may lead to a service and knowledge that others will value, cherish, and support.

(2) Do not underestimate the number or the commitment of people who may value and support you, your product, or your service, even in a place that outsiders may overgeneralize as being unsupportive or even hostile.

(3) Word of mouth is the best means to attract, retain, and grow a loyal and supportive following, including in a context where a specific subset of a larger population is the intended clientele or audience.

(4) When contracts and rule of law fail and people are dishonest—or, more generally, in a time of *any* hardship—reputation and relationships can sustain a person or an enterprise.

(5) Sometimes concentrating efforts on one location may reap greater rewards than a more diffuse presence.

(6) Carving out a portion of time for one's own health and time with family—whether we call this work–life balance or work–life harmony—is recommended as essential for maintaining peace of mind and happiness.

Chapter 3

Timor-Leste: Pride in Local Food and Hunger for Information after a Genocide

W ITHOUT SEARCHING ONLINE for the answer, how many of us could name the relatively new Portuguese-speaking Southeast Asian country where between 20–30 percent of the population was killed, tortured, disappeared, or became refugees following a 1975 invasion, then occupation, and then 1999 withdrawal by its neighbor's military?

The brutal and grizzly legacies of European colonialism and the Cold War help to understand the context of the two hopeful and positive stories in this chapter. One story is that of chef Cesar Trinito Freitas Gaio, the founder and owner of Dilicious Timor, who is bringing back pride in locally-sourced, healthy, and authentically Timorese food. The other is that of a team of journalists and an Australian who witnessed the aftermath of violence—and scrambled to set up the first news source—in the city of Dili after its information infrastructure was annihilated in 1999.

3.1. Entrance to Cesar Gaio's restaurant, Dilicious Timor, in Dili, Timor-Leste. (Image by Adam J. Sulkowski.)

The business climate: a result of history

The Indonesian Archipelago consists of over 17,500 islands. On the eastern tip of this island chain, north of Australia, is the island of Timor, which, thanks to its relative underdevelopment, is surrounded by some of the world's most pristine coral reefs. As the name suggests, most of Timor-Leste, or East Timor, is located on the eastern half of the island of Timor.

During the era of European colonialism, the Dutch colonized what is now Indonesia, and the Portuguese claimed this eastern part of Timor as theirs. The invasion and occupation of Japan during World War II is significant, in that it inspired the native population to coalesce, organize, and resist, at a cost of about

60,000 lives. After the Second World War, the Portuguese reestablished East Timor as a somewhat neglected "overseas province" until 1975, when a new government in Portugal ordered an abrupt withdrawal from—and decolonization of—its foreign territories.

Sudden independence may not have been a disaster for folks living in East Timor. But it was 1975. On the world stage, the United States had just retreated from Vietnam. The US and its allies could not abide by the possibility of newly independent East Timor becoming the Communist world's newest ally at the boundary of Southeast Asia and Oceania and the potential of a Soviet airbase being built within a ninety-minute bomber flight to Australia. In 1975, this seemed entirely possible.

Next door, America's ally in charge of Indonesia, a dictator—Suharto—worried that other islands in his archipelago might notice a newly independent East Timor and start their own independence movements. As a result of these fears, and backed with equipment from the United States and its allies, Indonesia invaded East Timor. According to documents released from the US National Security Archive in 2001, the invasion was personally greenlighted in a meeting between President Gerald Ford, Suharto, and Henry Kissinger, the American Secretary of State on the day before it commenced.

A murderous campaign against civilians ensued, claiming at least 100,000 lives in the short term. Precise statistics were not tracked. Masses of people fled villages and later could not be found. During much of the ensuing quarter-century of occupation, torture and terror were the standard tools for repressing the Timorese resistance.

Further devastation awaited at the end of twenty-four years of occupation. In 1999, while the rest of the world focused on the turn of the millennium, the local population was allowed a chance to vote on whether to remain a semiautonomous part of Indonesia or else to separate. When the East Timorese voted in favor of independence, Indonesian-backed militias killed over 15,000 more people in a final spasm of violence, creating a refugee population of over 200,000 and—according to eyewitnesses—completely leveling key infrastructure, including in the capital city of Dili.

3.2. A view from the coast of Dili, Timor-Leste. (Image by Adam J. Sulkowski.)

How the heck did I end up there?

East Timor had been one of those mysteries on the map. I wasn't familiar with the history described above, despite the last chapters of its history transpiring entirely during my lifetime. As long as I was in the area, I thought—next door in Indonesia—might as well hop onto a short flight and learn and figure things out once I got there.

Landing in Dili, I had my first inkling this place was different. The international airport is closer to the size and activity level of a local airstrip in the United States. As of my visit in 2018, I believe there may have been one or two flights a day linking Dili to the outside world. The most striking thing about landing at an airport where (A) rideshare apps don't work, (B) there aren't many taxi or tuk-tuk drivers waiting, and (C) you don't know the fair market price for getting into town, is that your brain automatically starts to look for friendly faces—anyone who might give a bit of good advice.

I'm not sure, but I think my eyes landed on his broadly-smiling face just before I heard his laughter and conversation with two people who were apparently leaving the country. Whoever this was, this guy seemed to be the friendliest-looking person in the lobby of the airport. When I asked for advice on getting into the city, the smiling fellow offered to give me a ride in his food truck, since he was headed into Dili anyway.

As it turns out, this was Cesar Gaio. A native of East Timor, he was educated as a chef overseas and then returned to solve a problem and pursue a mission. Although I had a vague plan of finding a place to stay and checking out the reefs, the conversation with Cesar immediately became interesting—so much so that I accepted an invitation to get lunch at his restaurant before doing anything else.

3.3. A food truck from Cesar Gaio's restaurant, Dilicious Timor, in Dili, Timor-Leste. (Image by Adam J. Sulkowski.)

The problem

Cesar's food truck and restaurant are more than businesses. They are his attempt to correct an atrocious absurdity. It turns out that over half of Timorese—especially in Dili—do not eat Timorese food. You'd guess that a tropical island could more than provide for itself with its own agriculture and seafood from surrounding waters. In fact, the oldest generations in the countryside still remember where and how to collect nutritious and wild vegetation. But most food is now imported and not even prepared according to local customs. This is not the first nor last time that I have run into this pattern.

One might attribute the erosion of native cultural traditions to colonialism. Past eras of colonialism are obviously a factor in East Timor, as they are elsewhere, as evidenced by Portuguese being the predominant language and by local religious norms. After all, over 90 percent of the population is Catholic, and one of the largest statues in the country (after one resembling the iconic Christ the Redeemer in Brazil) is a massive representation of Pope John Paul II at a mountaintop church, gesturing toward the capital. His visit in 1989 was noteworthy as the only one by a foreign head of state during the occupation. But the statue was a surreal sight and the last thing I expected to find in this remote corner of the world.

The legacy of past colonial eras and occupations is, however, not the main explanation for why people in the capital often don't consume food from their own country. A more recent and direct cause is free trade rules imposed on the country by the World Bank. These free trade rules require countries like East Timor, as a condition for loans and help, to open their markets to imports from abroad. Large Asian firms ship cheap and nutrient-poor white rice and noodles to East Timor, which are often considered better and more modern options. Even fish carried around by street merchants in Dili are often not caught by the merchants themselves off the shore—far more likely, they buy, carry around, and sell fish caught by large Chinese drift net trawlers further offshore.

The solution is Dilicious

Later, as I wrote-up the story of Cesar, I learned he'd been profiled online in 2016 in a BBC article about entrepreneurs in East Timor. The article described him as not yet able to afford a proper food truck. Instead, since 2015, he had operated a mobile kitchen, driving around with his locally-sourced ingredients and a propane stove. He used to set up and cook in different locations in his city. But by 2018, Cesar had a bigger truck and, with investments from two friends, was able to open a nice permanent location with indoor and patio seating.

3.4. Cesar Gaio and author Adam J. Sulkowski dining at Gaio's restaurant, Dilicious Timor, in Dili, Timor-Leste. (Image by Adam J. Sulkowski.)

His journey to becoming a cook and restaurateur

Cesar explained:

> I was lucky enough to have the opportunity to get a great education as a chef abroad. But I would not feel happy to stay somewhere else. There is something important to do here. We

have a culture. We should produce our own food. It's not right to import it from far away. It does not make sense—it's not good for the environment, it's not healthy for us . . . and, after our tough history, we should be proud of our own culture! This is why I had to come back, and I had to find a way. So, I came back and started preparing food. First, a little. Then I sold more and more. Now I have a food truck and this restaurant.

Besides preparing and serving delicious fish, vegetables, and juices, Cesar's restaurant, Dilicious Timor—a play on the word "delicious" and the name of the capital city, Dili—is memorable for two things. First, it features décor, glasses, and outdoor furniture made from repurposed discarded materials. There are also items for purchase crafted from discarded items like bottles. When I asked about the source of these, Cesar took me to a workshop down the street: a place where empty glass bottles are donated. There, people with impaired mobility cut the bottles, sand them, and sometimes decorate them to boost their value as glasses and gifts.

Over the past few decades, the idea of creating a circular economy has caught on around the world. In my experience, however, the greatest efficiency and best supply loops are sometimes found where even a glass bottle is seen as a valuable resource rather than something to discard. This is more likely to be the case in a place like East Timor, where the unemployment rate is around 20 percent and more than half of the population makes less than $1.25 per day.[1]

The second thing for which Dilicious Timor is memorable is

---

[1] Another example is in Puerto Iguazú, Argentina, where there is a family that built walls and furniture of an entire house from plastic bottles and other "waste" material.

that it is a great place to meet people. During my lunch with Cesar, he introduced me to someone who works at Dili's radio station, Luis Evaristo Soares—apparently a notable personality in East Timorese media—who would play a greater role in my visit than could have been foreseen based on our brief exchange of hellos, as explained in a subsequent section of this chapter.

3.5. Food served at Cesar Gaio's restaurant, Dilicious Timor, in Timor-Leste. (Image by Adam J. Sulkowski.)

The value of sharing where you are

Plenty of folks have deleted their social media profiles. It's easy to understand why: it can be a waste of time, and it's creepy how much information these platforms gather about us. But it can be useful to share where you are. Thanks to posting where I was, a friend somewhere else in the world noticed and put me in touch with an international development professional who'd moved to East Timor and had worked there, including in the countryside, for eight years.

It was invaluable to hear the development professional's observations, as an outsider with years of local experience, confirming what others had shared about the country, its history, and current challenges. And thanks to her urging, I visited a museum documenting the years of Indonesian occupation, which is located in a former prison. Like other such sites in the world, it is powerful and unforgettable.

The value of showing up and of not forgetting brief introductions

In my last few hours before leaving East Timor, I dropped by a conference I had seen advertised: an international forum on freedom of the press at the gleaming new Ministry of Finance. At first, the guards said there was no chance of getting through the gates of the fenced-off compound. Their stated reason was that I was wearing shorts rather than trousers.

I lingered, and was rewarded by the sight of Luis Soares—the person I'd met at Cesar's restaurant a few days earlier—stepping out of a car just on the other side of the gates. "Hello!" I waved.

"Ah, you! Why don't you come inside?" Luis said.

"I can't! These guys say shorts are not allowed!" I replied. A quick wave from Luis and a few words in Portuguese were enough. The guards opened the gate. Luis asked what brought me to the conference. "Well, I got this crazy idea for a book," I replied. "I keep running into people with amazing stories, who do things that don't seem easy. Any chance there's someone with a story here?" By now, we were inside.

"That guy," Luis said, pointing. "When this session ends, I'll introduce you."

3.6. A banner at the site of an international forum on freedom of the press held in Dili, Timor-Leste, in July 2018. (Image by Adam J. Sulkowski.)

The Y2K problem, journalists, an Aussie, and satisfying a hunger for information

Luis was right. The story of how Bob Howarth, consultant to Timorese journalists and Australian media, improvised a newspaper operation in a destroyed city has all the elements of an *Extreme Entrepreneurship* story: resourcefulness despite (or because of) lacking resources and inspiration springing from desperation. What follows is a synopsis of Bob's account.

It was early 2000. The international journalist community

called for assistance in East Timor in the wake of the violence there. Bob, a technology manager at the time for a newspaper in Brisbane, Australia, was asked by the University of Queensland to help thirteen visiting Timorese journalists who had just completed training on how to report in post-conflict environments (run by the Reuters Kosovo bureau chief).

The immediate problem: not a single working computer was left in Dili in 2000

As it so happened, the headquarters of Bob's newspaper was about to pay to dispose of computers deemed faulty due to the Y2K or Millennium bug (a suspected glitch related to the formatting of calendar data starting in the year 2000). So, Bob easily negotiated getting the computers for free. This solved the first problem. But plenty of obstacles remained.

How to get used computers to Dili?

Bob arranged, in exchange for positive publicity, for a newspaper in Darwin, Australia to complete the shipment of the computers to Dili. He arrived with the equipment to find a city still in smoking ruins and patrolled by UN peacekeepers. Once there, Bob met journalist friends, including Hugo da Costa, who would become the founding Editor-in-Chief of a new newspaper, and Santina Santos, Rosa Garcia, Jose Ximenes, and twelve others dedicated to restoring access to news and information.

The next problem: there was no reliable power source

The team got approval from the Australian contingent of peace-keepers to jerry-rig a power line from the Australian camp's generator to what was about to become the office of the *Timor*

Post. Working in sauna-like conditions and fending off a curious stray pig that had somehow escaped the recent carnage, the journalists gathered and prepared news summaries. They joked that they were using the "sneaker-net" to transfer text and images to the page designer's computer—meaning they had to carry documents on floppy disks.

The first edition of the *Timor Post* would include a page in Portuguese and one in English, plus ten in Tetum, the language of Timor—a world first, apparently, for a newspaper. The inaugural issue had to be published within forty-eight hours on the day the Indonesian president was slated to visit Dili to apologize for recent events. The team knew it was a "must" to spread the word to the city about that, and about other recent events in Timor-Leste.

3.7. Bob Howarth and journalists gathered around a computer, in Dili, Timor-Leste. (Image courtesy of Bob Howarth.)

One final hurdle: there was no working printer left in Dili

With time running out before their self-imposed deadline, Bob noticed something in the office of the manager of the construction camp-style hotel at which he was sleeping—a shiny new printer. A deal was struck. The manager would allow the free printing of this "newspaper" if Bob provided the toner cartridge and paper. Bob ended up buying whatever ink and paper he could find in the city. Several hundred copies of the pages were printed and stapled together and ready to distribute.

The image that sticks with me: hunger for information

The image of Bob's story that stuck in my mind was this: his team driving around a devastated Dili, yelling and throwing out free copies of the city's first post-conflict "newspaper" on stapled A3 office paper. People were so hungry for a credible source of information that they ran into the streets and fought to grab and read these precious pages. This image is all the more poignant when one considers that many Timorese cannot read well—a high illiteracy rate continues to be a stubborn legacy of past eras. After food, shelter, and safety, this recounted image indicates that other primal human needs are connectedness and information.

Back to the present era

As shared at the conference at which I met Luis and Bob, according to Reporters Sans Frontières, Timor-Leste has recently enjoyed the highest World Press Freedom ranking in Asia—95th in the world, as listed in the organization's World Press Freedom Index in 2018. In 2020, the *Timor Post* celebrated its 20th anniversary, now one of four daily newspapers in this country of about 1.3 million people. As elsewhere, the printed news sources struggle to generate enough advertising revenue to survive, and the press council and others have been considering the establishment of a fact-checking system.

East Timor avoided major disruptions from the 2020–2021 COVID-19 pandemic by shutting its borders early. There had been, as of the end of the year 2020, only thirty cases of COVID-19, and all of these people fully recovered. During 2020, Cesar secured a lease of a second property, and he has been preparing to open a second restaurant.

Takeaway lessons that could help you in other situations in life and business

(1) The failures of trade systems may create opportunities.

(2) The re-localization of supply chains can result in healthier food options.

(3) Restoring local pride in traditions can be constructive and the basis of a business.

(4) Waste in one context can be a valuable asset in another context.

(5) Local and international networks may be willing to help rapidly when asked.

(6) Even in a crisis, people have a fundamental need for connection and information.

(7) As illustrated in other stories in this book, there is a balance between planning and having a predisposition toward ac-

tion—with most of the protagonists having a stronger bias toward acting. In this chapter, similarly, my instinct to go and explore without a plan (a case of "winging it") had an outsized return on invested time and resources—more learned in less time than in other cases where I invested ten-times more in research and prepping.

(8) Another lesson (echoed in the entrepreneurs' stories in these chapters) is to say hi and ask if someone's open to helping you. Don't assume universal indifference or hostility. If you're trying to do something positive, a lot of folks may want to help.

(9) Social media usage definitely can have negative impacts—but as this chapter illustrates, sharing your location can sometimes lead to invaluable introductions or suggestions.

(10) Finally: go—show up—including to that somewhat random conference in town. It is almost cliché to say that the biggest factor in success is showing up, or that there is magic in taking the first step. But the backstories in this chapter, on how I met Cesar and then Bob, illustrate these truths.

Chapter 4

Guatemala: Broke to Smuggler to Legal Exporter of Ilegal Mezcal

A BROKE TRAVELER did not set out to build a distinctive brand in a crowded global market that has a total value of over half a trillion dollars and is dominated by big established companies. Rather, John Rexer's café, bookstore, and bar in Antigua, Guatemala (plus his business distributing mezcal to the United States under the brand Ilegal Mezcal) show what a blend of desperation and creative impulses can eventually produce after sixteen years of work.

First disclaimer: I almost didn't include this story, because I don't want, as a law professor, to be perceived to be encouraging law-breaking or intoxication. Suffice it to say that my youngest brother died in an incident involving alcohol—a fact I always mention to my temporarily immortal-feeling students. So, please be careful and temperate if you choose to imbibe. But ultimately, John's story is so entertaining, thought-provoking, funny at times, and instructional that I have to include it. Enjoy responsibly.

Second disclaimer: more so than is the case with the other stories in this book, I had no way of verifying every detail that follows.

4.1. The Santa Catalina Arch, in Antigua, Guatemala. (Image by Adam J. Sulkowski.)

How to get money when you are broke?

The bar, Café No Sé, was John's first business and was actually born out of a combination of spur-of-the-moment impulse, having no resources, and improvising in a key moment of opportunity. John had left the US in the early 2000s, explaining he'd "had enough" of the politics of post-9/11 America. He had backpacked through Mexico and Central America and, in 2003, found himself broke and looking for shelter in a downpour in Antigua.

An elderly gentleman asked John if he would like to come in and potentially rent his building, and he invited John in for a tour. Just to get out of the drenching rain, John agreed. Inside the colonial-era walls, the space was a dilapidated workshop, in shambles and filled with scrap parts and material.

As John tells the story:

To this day, I still don't know where this came from, but I

said: "Great, I'll take it, and I'll put a bar in front." The problem was, really, I didn't have a penny left. Even the credit card I had was so worn out and melted that it wouldn't work. Again, I really don't know where this idea came from—I said: "Look . . . but . . . I have business partners, and they have conditions. They won't agree to pay first month's rent, and actually, there's a lot of work to do to set up, so we won't be able to pay rent for the first two months, and we cannot pay a damage deposit."

I had no business partners, but it sounded better than admitting I was broke. Also, I had a few drinks in me. Divine inspiration, as it were. He agreed to deferring payments for a few months, and I agreed to whatever he'd asked for in terms of monthly rent, on a handshake, not having a clue if it was fair market rate or not.

A matter of minutes later, a couple showed up and explained that, having been suddenly displaced out of their salsa dance studio, they were looking for a new location. They begged to tour the site to which John had just been introduced.

Again, in John's words:

The elderly gentleman smiled and said, "No sé (I don't know), it's up to this gringo here, talk to him"—pointing to me. So, I find myself giving a tour of a location I had literally, a matter of minutes earlier, first seen. They said, "Perfect—we'd love to put the salsa studio here in front."

I said, "Wait, hold on, that's where my bar will be. You can have the back, but . . . look . . . my partners have strict conditions: we'll need two months' rent up front and a damage deposit." They agreed to the same rate that I had been offered—

half of the total for their share of the space, with the first payments and the damage deposit due immediately. Again, I still had no idea if it was a fair rate—but I now had some money to start something here."

John had a location and startup capital. Other than that, he had nearly no other assets, except for his knowledge—from his time vagabonding through the region—about small farmers in Southern Mexico producing small batches of mezcal for personal use or local sale—unregulated, uninspected, and not certified for export.

Time-out: how I got to meet John

Before we continue with a description of how John grew his businesses, the way we met bears mention. Having taught a class on intellectual property law on a morning in March 2017, in Boston, I made it onto a sequence of flights that got me to Antigua, Guatemala the same day, after dark. My hostel was locked. A guy was sleeping outside so peacefully that it seemed impolite to wake him up by knocking. Plus, across the street, painted on a wall, was a name that had caught my eye in a guidebook: *Café No Sé. Huh*, I thought. *What luck. It's not that late. Why not check it out?*

To set the scene: Café No Sé, John's office, and his bookstore and café are on a cobblestone-paved colonial street. Antigua is one of those 400-plus-year-old Spanish-built cities where the exteriors of buildings have not been modernized much. Arriving at night, it's easy to imagine you've stepped into another decade, another era, or another century. None of the businesses in that area had signs protruding into the street to catch your eye. There's just a door and words painted on the wall outside.

Inside Café No Sé, it's small, hazy, cozy, candle-lit, and always—every night—there was (until the pandemic starting in

2020) live music in the first room, across from the first bar. In the back is a second bar (and further back, I'd later learn, is John's office, labeled "Bad Idea Factory"). I'd also later learn that the refrigerator door in the second room was not a decoration but rather that it opened to reveal a mezcal bar with nothing but small-batch mezcals, informally brought in from Mexico. It was these mezcals that gave this business its notoriety and, as described later in this story, was one of the reasons for the memorable choice of name for John's mezcal brand.

Upon my entering the bar and sliding up to the counter, an expat told me a story about the founder, John Rexer, dressing as a priest to smuggle mezcal from Mexico into Guatemala. Then he pointed: "That's him in the corner." So, that night was my introduction to both John and the smoky liquor made from the distilled heart of agave, mezcal, made in Southern Mexico (related to but distinct from tequila, and not related at all to the similar-sounding hallucinogen mescaline).

The next day, John agreed to meet and speak with me. Distilled (pun intended) from three hours of walking and talking, the following sections of this chapter are the highlights of our conversation.

4.2. Outside view of the entrance to John Rexer's bar, Café No Sé, in Antigua, Guatemala. (Image by Adam J. Sulkowski.)

4.3. Bottles of mezcal lining a shelf at John Rexer's bar, Café No Sé, in Antigua, Guatemala. (Image by Adam J. Sulkowski.)

4.4. The entrance to John Rexer's office at his bar, Café No Sé, in Antigua, Guatemala. (Image by Adam J. Sulkowski.)

What was it like starting out?

"I had no f'ing clue what to do," John started. When John said he had run out of money, he really meant it. He had to turn the cash from his subletters into a profit quickly, but he had more obstacles than a short runway. "When the owner showed me the place," he explained, "there were piles of junk—it was a dump—one of those places to weld chicken buses. I slept here, at the age of forty-three, a backpack under my head, in front. I didn't know anyone here yet. I could have called friends back in New York and borrowed money, but I didn't want to be in debt to anyone."

John continued: "Also, I didn't have enough money to do this legally. It would cost $1,200 to get licenses. But then again, the town was relatively lawless then. At first, I passed bottles through the window in the door to people willing to pay, while I frantically figured out how to turn beautiful junk into a bar and furniture with a handsaw and a hammer."

Once Café No Sé opened, John described a not atypical startup grind of "falling asleep at 2 a.m. and waking up at 5 a.m." and living "hand to mouth." There was also some regulatory uncertainty, besides initially not having a permit: "A year before, there had been a purging of bars. For a while, only beer and wine were officially permitted to be sold and consumed. One solution was serving liquor in a mug with a string of teabags. I wrote on the menu, 'Ask about our special white tea.' When [clients] did [ask], I'd say, 'Under the bar we have gin, vodka, rum, tequila. [But] I have to serve it in a teacup.'"

Was there a vision for Café No Sé?

"I knew I wanted live music," John responded. "At first, musicians would meet, gather, and practice in back. But no, there was no vision. But I knew it would evolve into a funky Petri dish of romantic souls."

How would you respond if someone critiqued the business saying that you're making money from a substance that is addictive and can end up causing harm?

"Bars are important. People meet. They exchange ideas. This is not a place where we shake people upside down and take all their money. There's a community here."

What's the secret to creating an atmosphere that becomes world-famous out of an old workshop?

"A bar is not a place," John explained. "It's the people. Including the people who work here. Bartending skills are not that important to me. My customers can attest to that. I don't hire based on bartending skills. What I do hire for is someone able to talk: [someone] who understands things from the other side of the bar, who knows how to ignite conversation and introduce one customer to another. Good energy, but also won't take s**t from anyone. A bar is a world of characters, so you should not try to control the chemistry of the room unless things get boring. It should be a place for the bungled, botched, and brilliant."

What about the bookstore and café?

"The place adjacent to No Sé was bright blue, yellow, and fluorescent. An Internet café. I hated it. My landlord wanted to rent it to me. I said if you take out all the damn computers, I'll rent it. I was still broke, not thinking. Just moving, got to get it done."

What ties Café No Sé together?

"A couple from California once asked, 'What is your concept?' Simple: I put all my vices under one roof—live music, poker, booze, a dash of madness, and later books and coffee—and hoped people would show up."

How did Café No Sé become known in some circles as one of the world's best dive bars?

"It was discovered in about 2005. Writers and journalists were passing through. We got overrun with politics that year. The bar became a journalist hangout."

What's with this story about smuggling mezcal from Mexico?

"So, I built this place," John began. "I wanted something like an agave, mezcal, tequila bar. But for that, I needed good Mexican spirits. And I knew from traveling through Mexico about this great mezcal that small-time farmers made in their backyard distilleries which they call palenques.

"I went up to Mexico, to villages, buying mezcal by taste and production methods that appealed to me, sometimes in bottles, or putting it in five-liter gas cans. I'd write notes about the taste and origins and attach those, bringing twenty to thirty liters back over the border. This matters. The quality of mezcal can vary from palenque to palenque significantly. I got to know who took pride in their craft. It's all in the details."

John explained that Café No Sé's mezcal is "made in Oaxaca—either a twenty-four-hour trip by bus or about twelve hours in total by car." Because these were literally backyard stills, and totally unregulated, it was important to know the sources and who had good practices. So, yes, we started bringing small batches down informally. We started to serve more and more mezcal. People loved it, and they loved the stories of how it got here."

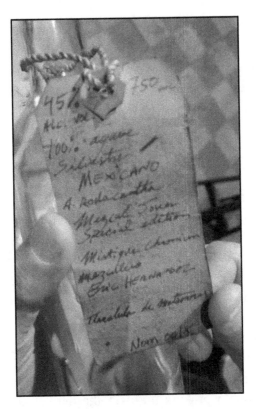

4.5. A label hanging from a bottle of mezcal at John Rexer's bar, Café No Sé, in Antigua, Guatemala, showing his notes on taste and origins of the mezcal in the bottle. (Image by Adam J. Sulkowski.)

What are your best stories about smuggling mezcal?

"You have to remember this has been one of the most corrupt borders in the world. Everyone looks to either extort or steal from you: border guards on the river, military, police, gangs, and thieves. At first, we were bringing in several bottles in duffel bags pretending it was personal luggage and just hoping no one would inspect carefully or else rob us. But even then, it was a day and a half by bus to get to Oaxaca, plus several days of running between villages to collect mezcal before the day and a half trip back. Not an efficient way to stock a bar."

What is this about dressing as a priest?

John told the story: "Once, I was coming back from Mexico, at the official border crossing with my friend Lucas with about fifteen duffle bags with maybe sixty bottles of mezcal. We stopped at a market to get some clothing—any cheap stuff—to conceal the bubble-wrapped bottles of mezcal in our luggage. Lucas is a romantic madman—a painter and musician who resembles Salvador Dali, with a pencil-thin mustache and, as I was about to discover, a weakness for porn. He was more than a bit tipsy from sampling some of the mezcal that we'd procured. So, there I am, at the Mexican-Guatemalan border with contraband and a drunk man resembling Zorro on my hands.

"Lucas saw a priest's outfit in the market and said that I should buy it and put it on: 'who's going to challenge a priest?' he asked. It seemed like a good idea. In fact, we did get through the checkpoint on the Mexican side of the river very smoothly.

"Continuing to customs on the Guatemalan side, Drunk Zorro got through without a hitch. But a border guard stopped me and asked what was in my duffle bags. I replied: 'Regalos para mis amigos y libros para los niños' (gifts for my friends and books for the children).

"The border guard stared at me, and then pointed to one of my bags and ordered: 'Abra su maleta' (open your bag). Of course, I complied. At first, I thought this was not a problem, because we had stuffed plenty of clothes and books at the top of the bag to conceal the mezcal underneath. But my friend had not told me that, back in Mexico, he had made a last-minute purchase of porn and shoved it in, at the top of this bag. There they were, hardcore porn mags, staring back at the border guard and me, in my priestly attire, and both of us equally shocked.

"The border guard let out a breath and looked up at me: 'Que es eso?' (What is this?) I was sweating, and my knees were shaking. I repeated: 'Regalos para mis amigos y libros para los niños.' Another long moment passed before I asked: 'Esta bien?' He shook his head laughing and waved me through: 'Esta bien, Padre. Esta bien. Pasale. Pasale. (It's ok, Father. It's ok. Pass. Go ahead.)' Fifty percent of the time I was terrified doing this kind of thing. I was raised a good Catholic boy."

4.6. John Rexer sits on a stool at his bar, Café No Sé, in Antigua, Guatemala. (Image courtesy of John Rexer.)

How did you keep up with demand once you started selling more?

"We had to get creative when demand increased. We either had to find people with whom to work, or else just avoided trouble by going around the official crossing. The first time that someone offered to sell a whole pallet, and I said there was no way I could sneak hundreds of bottles across, he smiled and said, 'No te preocupes, yo tengo un tío'—meaning 'Don't worry about it, I have an uncle.'

"Sure enough, when we got to the river, there was a warehouse with everything in it you can imagine and rafts built of inner tubes and wooden slats. You could get anything across that river—anything. You can still get an elephant across the river and avoid the official crossing. But it was still a desperate experience, slogging through mud on the other side, guns everywhere, fearing or knowing we'd be ripped off."

As someone who teaches law, I gotta ask—any regrets about taking part in smuggling?

"What if there's more crime, corruption, and risk of violence doing it the legal way?" John pointed out. "Again, this is one of the more corrupt borders in the world. Years later, when we got mezcal certified for export, we would try to do it legally. It could be more corrupt, dangerous, and result in a total loss. What if you pay a tax or fee at the border, and the border guard radios friends, and thirty minutes later you're held-up by a policeman who also wants mordida, a bribe? And next, a bandit is tipped off and you get extorted again or get completely robbed at gunpoint? That happened to us more than once.

"Many times, we tried to do it legally, officially. And we got jacked—a total loss. So, what if there's less crime and less risk of robbery and violence by avoiding the legal route? What if, the other way, you pay a fee once, and you're done? When what is ostensibly legal is corrupt, should you be a boy scout?"

It is a great brand name—"Ilegal"—did you partly do the smuggling to justify the name later, knowing you would eventually go into business exporting it?

"No, the smuggling at the beginning was out of desperation and necessity. I was a broke bar owner with a supply problem—it wasn't part of a premeditated plan to make as much money as possible. Also, the name 'Ilegal' was partly inspired by people from the communities where we buy the mezcal. Many have loved ones that have gone, out of desperation, since there were no jobs available locally, to the US to work as undocumented laborers. As we all know, they're wrongly referred to as 'illegal' too. These are people with whom we work. I thought about the name 'Ilegal' a lot. It's also a nod to them and hints at concerns a lot of people share related to immigration reform, borders, surveillance, and freedom."

Did it ever cross your mind, though, in the early days: "This will justify a cool, edgy, naughty-sounding name someday later, if I export this stuff?"

"No, I was just waking up every morning in a fevered sweat, thinking: *how am I going to get this bar to survive.*"

Are there still mornings like that?

"All the time! In 2006 and again in 2014–2015, I put up the bar as collateral to borrow money to keep the mezcal business alive. We were down to our last $80,000, not exporting much. Competing on an international stage is exceedingly expensive, and you lose money for several years in the hope of building a successful brand. Then, and more importantly, there is also the importance of paying a fair price for mezcal and the hard, manual labor that goes into producing it.

"From an early stage, I thought about economic sustainability for the distillers we work with, which means not just paying good wages but providing them with consistent year-round business. I reiterate, this is a very expensive field of endeavor. It requires investors, and when we began, few had faith in mezcal. Now, I do not wake up in a fevered sweat, because I never sleep."

When was the first inkling you would go from smuggling small amounts to creating an export business?

"I saw people loving the taste of mezcal—the varieties, the stories, the history. By 2006 or 2007, people were coming to the bar specifically requesting mezcal. When mixologists from New York, Los Angeles, Chicago, and London started emailing me about mezcal, I knew we had something.

"I was lucky to be one of the earlier foreigners to have built relationships with *mezcaleros* who made fine mezcal. I thought: if we are going to do this—meaning build a brand for export—we are going to figure this out ourselves and do it well. We'll also do all the creative parts of branding and the difficult part of education about the category, as well as the sales. I would tell those working with me that we have *tabula rasa*, so we have both an opportunity and an obligation to try and do this right."

The export business—how did you go from smuggling mezcal to getting it certified for export to bringing it out legally, and what else did you do to sell mezcal in the US?

"The process took a lot of time: sending samples to government laboratories, getting trademarks in Mexico and other countries, and getting certification for quality under what was then the newly-formed regulatory body for mezcal called COMERCAM (now called the CRM). Mezcal has *denomination of origin* similar to Cognac and Champagne, which means mezcal is specific to a country and region. The only place in the world mezcal can be produced is Mexico. Oaxaca and seven other Mexican states are certified under the CRM. Then, with certification, you can export legally to a place like the United States. The process of securing intellectual property rights has cost the company roughly $500,000—probably more."

Almost half a million dollars? Just for IP? How big is this operation now, selling mezcal around the US?

"About fifty people now work for Ilegal assisting in distribution, marketing, and branding. We now sell in about twenty-five countries, with the US being the biggest market. In 2019, we sold about 27,500 nine-liter cases. This may sound like a lot, but in the world of spirits, we are still quite small.

"As we grow, the promise of our company is to stay true to quality, small-batch, and artisanal production and put economic and environmental sustainability at the forefront of all we do. The last thing we want to do is destroy the beautiful spirit and harm in any way the culture that produces it. We will never industrialize our mezcal or rush the process. But we have the ability to grow over time by hiring more people and adding more artisanal 200-liter copper stills with the two partner distillers we work with in Oaxaca."

You mentioned Bacardi made an investment in Ilegal Mezcal?

"Yes. They bought a minority stake in our company in 2015. Some people freaked out about it because Bacardi is a multinational liquor company with many commercial brands. The fear was that we would become industrial. Nothing could be further from the truth. Bacardi values how our mezcal is produced, realizing that the truly handcrafted nature is what sets mezcal apart from other spirits. Part of our agreement is that our artisanal production methods will not change. Where Bacardi has been a huge help is providing a route to national distribution, which is very difficult for a small brand to obtain without a major industry partner."

Do you worry that any of what you do at Café No Sé—the bar's character—will get ruined if Ilegal gets too much attention? What about Ilegal Mezcal: will it get ruined if it becomes too mass-market, too popular?

"About our bar and customers: we attract self-selecting visitors, with a different way of thinking. This is a huge generalization, but there is a very real sense of community. We're small and communal yet international. A somewhat dark underbelly. Educated folks who dropped out because they wanted community—a human interaction. Kill your preconceptions.

"As for Ilegal, well, for a liquor brand to survive, it has to become somewhat mass market. The attrition rate in the liquor business is staggering. Hundreds, perhaps thousands of brands perish every year. If we maintain our quality by producing artisanally, and if we keep to our values of social and environmental responsibility, then commercial growth is a very good thing. We will be able to provide more quality jobs in Oaxaca and perhaps in some small way set an example of what a better business model is. The other thing is that Ilegal is not just a commodity, it is a culture built around community, music, travel, literature. It is, in many ways, a way of thinking. I often say it is not a 'lifestyle' but a glorious 'death style' since we are all headed in that direction anyway."

You mentioned politics and community. This might be the moment to explain the political ad you used to promote Ilegal Mezcal and how it went viral.

[Note: Whether a reader loves the message or hates it, John's ad is interesting because it is hard to intentionally plan a campaign to organically go viral. Sorry in advance if the following story offends your political sensibilities or sense of propriety, but this seems worth including.]

"I went back to visit family in 2015, to New York City," John recalls. "We're at a restaurant, and when the waiter came over, I asked him where he was from. He told me Puebla, Mexico. I told him how much I loved Puebla, that I had lived there many years back, that I loved the food, the town. The waiter said to me, 'It's good to know everyone is not like Trump.' Then he said, 'Donald es un pendejo' (Donald is an a**hole). I thought this is probably how many Mexicans felt at that moment. Then I thought of all the hard-working Mexicans we work with on both sides of the border.

"Very spontaneously, without thought of repercussion or even thinking of this as an ad campaign, I decided to paste thousands of posters around Manhattan and Brooklyn with a silhouette of Trump, reading *Donald, Eres Un Pendejo* [followed by the text *The Only Thing That Should Be Ilegal Is Mezcal*]. I used 'eres' instead of 'es' for emphasis: 'Donald, You are an a**hole.' We later did giant graffiti projections on buildings with the same image. Think of images the size of Batman's bat signal. It went crazy viral."

I saw that on Business Insider some time ago. You must have gotten millions of dollars in free advertising for Ilegal Mezcal. And that wasn't planned?

"It was an impulse. Sometimes an impulse gets you into trouble! But instant death is doing things by committee. Viscerally, I knew . . . this felt right. . . . It was just: 'Let's go, this is great.' My attitude is: 'As long as we are all racing headlong into the abyss, might as well take [a] chance [to] stand and fight for something, feel alive, get some good stories.'"

What do you think of the whole sustainability movement?

"Everyone talks about sustainability. There is a lot of lip service paid to it, and often, it is just a marketing blurb. Often people either have idealized or cynical ideas of what is needed for the developing world.

"From a business point of view, in terms of what we are doing with mezcal, there needs to be volume to have an impact in terms of economic sustainability. Piecemeal, very sporadic work does not provide secure income and leads to migration. Whole villages in Oaxaca were decimated in the 1980s and 90s due to lack of jobs and low wages. People fled to the US to look for work.

"Moreover, you cannot build a business if those who work with you are financially insecure. Economic stability means providing secure jobs and good wages. It's both the right thing to do and good business. Our goal is to grow in tandem with our distillers so that they know we will be here in twenty years and that they, too, will be here. It has to be beneficial for both parties long-term.

"As to environmental sustainability, well, I mentioned before that we had *tabula rasa*—a chance from the start to do things correctly. We are fortunate that we have the ability to look at best practices from many industries, be it coffee producers, fisheries, forestry, and of course well-run distilleries. Alongside the mezcaleros we work with, we have begun to employ practices to recycle water, reforest the certified wood we use for distillation, eliminate plastic and other non-recyclables, etcetera."

Final reflections

My conversation with John turned a bit philosophical, contemplating the big problems in the world and how to make sense of—and act in—systems that often seem broken and corrupt. He explained: "I make a living doing the best with what I know about the world. There's cognitive dissonance sometimes, but you do the best you can in the Petri dish you are in. Or you compartmentalize. It's easy to become a modern-day sociopath: those people sometimes seem to be the most successful. We tell kids, 'Here are morals,' and then we check what we told kids—our values—at the door of work. Society sometimes rewards checking morals at the door, teaching you to be amoral, not to really care."

John continued: "Money is secondary. It is lower down the totem pole. It is actually the biggest impediment to creativity, to doing well. When you have nothing—no capital—you see what is there and make something of it. You have to be resourceful, and that is the fun. The resourcefulness becomes infectious, and you make an amazing connection with other people who want to join in the creativity.

"It is harder now than before, but there are still opportunities. There is social or peer pressure that demands that you are successful quickly. But then you are just money-driven. That can leave things horribly soulless. The last thing we want is to live in a world that is purely mercantile and mercenary."

Takeaway lessons that could help you in other situations in life and business

(1) Desperation and impulse can sometimes be steered constructively.

(2) We cannot tell when or where inspiration will strike, but following creative gut instincts can sometimes produce "outlier" results, where a safer decision-by-deliberative-process would have resulted in a much less interesting story.

(3) When startup capital is nonexistent and credit is unavailable, defer cash outflows and take cash upfront for whatever can be sold, rented out, or sublet.

(4) Hire for disposition and personality characteristics that cannot be taught or imparted—skills are secondary and can be acquired.

(5) Build upon whatever makes you or your service unique.

(6) Scaling-up and creating a business that is sustainable economically can give you credibility and influence to encourage environmentally- and societally-positive changes.

(7) Money is not the only or primary motive to keep pursuing a business, and a rollercoaster of emotions and ethical ambiguities are a part of an entrepreneur's journey.

(8) As in some of the other chapters of this book, both John's story and the backstory of how we met are, again, examples of a balance between some planning (or background knowledge), being aware of and engaged in what is around "in the moment," and being open to serendipitous opportunities.

Chapter 5

Madagascar: Empowering Local Economies in Villages with Solar Mini-Grid 3.0

"**D**ON'T WORRY, WE KNOW it's precious, we got this," said a Malagasy villager, one of about three dozen unloading one-ton pallets of solar panels and equipment by hand from a tractor-trailer. The odds of a disastrous drop seemed 50/50. In contrast to my doubts, the project leaders seemed confident that the equipment would all be safely unloaded and used to complete a solar-powered mini-grid. Beyond that, they seemed sure that selling access to electricity in Marosely, a village of about 2,500 people, would make enough money to pay for itself and even return some money to investors.

Camille André-Bataille, Co-CEO of ANKA Madagascar, provided the explanation to me. Camille was one of several women entrepreneurs and a total of over fifty-five native Malagasy and expat sources (known as *Vazaha* if they happen to be light-skinned) with whom I spoke in the summer of 2019. Some were brutally candid about the challenges of starting a business in a neocolonial economy where the legal system doesn't always work as it should. But Camille sees a way forward, as imagined and now jointly realized with her Co-CEO, Nico Livache.

This chapter describes the adaptations needed by a business to bring electricity to rural Madagascar, where 90–95 percent of people in villages are not on any power grid.

5.1. Malagasy villagers unload a crate of solar panels from a truck, in the village of Marosely, Madagascar. (Image by Adam J. Sulkowski.)

How I ended up there

Never underestimate the power of saying "hi" to strangers. In case you didn't notice in the last few chapters, that is a recurring theme of this book. On a cold nighttime run during a sleet storm along the Charles River in Boston in the winter of 2019, someone ran past me with music blaring from a backpack festooned with colored lights. Several runners followed. It was apparently one of those running groups that give each other mutual support. Long story short, I ended up chatting with one runner in the group who shared that he invests in places where other people do not and that he was off to, among other places, Madagascar to see how his investments were doing.

His name is Eric Klose. He was an early employee of Wayfair who cashed out and started his own investment firm, Ground Squirrel Ventures. This name is a deliberate attempt to humorously contrast himself and his focus from firms with grander names like Sequoia. Eric's mission is to make small investments in places even riskier than what are sometimes called "frontier markets"—places where inconsistent rule of law and $1 per day incomes are the norm. Eric's goal is to show others that investments in these markets into locally-run startups can generate returns, improve lives in the communities where they operate, and are worth the risk.

Fast forward several months and planning emails and Eric and I met in Cape Town, South Africa, near the southern tip of the African continent. We toured an incubator for startups located in a former prison and met local investors and entrepreneurs before traveling onward to Madagascar.

Background on Madagascar

Madagascar is a large island off the East Coast of Africa. Because of its size and isolation, it is sometimes called Earth's eighth continent. It is home to a large number of plant and animal species that exist nowhere else. These include different kinds of lemurs, chameleons, and critters with great names such as the aye-aye, fossa, and satanic leaf-tailed gecko. The future of its land-based and coastal ecosystems is uncertain, given that the vast majority of Madagascar has been deforested and large-scale fishing has increased offshore by Africa's latest neocolonial exploiter, China. The first humans in Madagascar are thought to have arrived from Polynesia. Since then, people have come from Africa, India, the Middle East, and eventually Europe.

As we'll soon learn, it is important to understand that a lot of Madagascar's economy does not function primarily for the benefit of the average citizen of Madagascar—known as Malagasy. To understand that, it helps to know that Madagascar was a French colony from the end of the nineteenth century until 1960 and that this still very much affects the realities of today. For example, much of the economy is still oriented around producing agricultural commodities like vanilla for export, even as child malnutrition is rampant.

Getting to the village of Marosely

As a first-time visitor from abroad, landing in the capital of Madagascar, Antananarivo (or Tana as it is commonly called), one can't help noticing a few things, including the rice fields on the way into the city center and the remarkable views, thanks to the city being located on a set of hills in the highlands, which can make the nights chilly. Eric and I had scheduled some meetings at a business school named Institut Superieur de la Communication, des Affaires et du Management—or ISCAM. Amusing acronym (to an English-speaker) notwithstanding, through them we were put in touch with local entrepreneurs with some promising businesses involving the local food economy, described later in this chapter.

Getting to the village of Marosely meant flying to the island of Nosy Be in the north (on an airline affectionately nicknamed "Air Maybe") and taking a local ferry back to the mainland, and then a trip by van along a paved road to a dirt road and crossing a tidal estuary (pictured at the end of this section) to Marosely—which, at last check, does not appear on Google Maps. It was in this village that, through incredible luck, we happened to be visiting when a very unpredictable delivery of solar panels arrived. Villagers there in Marosely then self-organized to unload heavy pallets of fragile equipment, as described and pictured at the opening of this chapter.

5.2. A truck crossing a tidal estuary on the road to the village of Marosely, Madagascar. (Image by Adam J. Sulkowski.)

Mini-Grid 3.0: incubating local (client) businesses

"We are the first and only mini-grid builder in Madagascar and one of a very few in the world (as far as we know) who is taking an approach that we may call Mini-Grid 3.0, meaning we are—based on local consultations—siting solar power generation and electricity distribution, plus also providing support—and even space sometimes—for local businesses," Camille, the Co-CEO of ANKA Madagascar, explained. Until now, essential services—including basic medical care and food processing and preservation—could not be provided locally due to lack of adequate electric power. Essential activities have been costlier, less safe, and worse for the environment because they required transportation of material or people to and from a city.

In a very real sense, reliable access to electric power can mean the difference between life and death. Pictured at the end of this section is a birthing bed inside the local health clinic. If someone is sick or injured or needing help with something like giving birth, one's options are to use this clinic or else risk a trip, possibly by animal-drawn carriage, into the nearest city that may have better facilities available. Incubating new local businesses and helping existing village activities to adopt electricity can therefore save and improve lives, reduce waste and environmental harms such as pollution from transportation, and result in paying customers that can allow the mini-grid to be financially viable.

5.3. A birthing bed at a health clinic, in the village of Marosely, Madagascar. (Image by Adam J. Sulkowski.)

Why so confident of success and that people will pay?

Whether it is in a failing state, emerging market, family business, or where I teach in the Boston area, aspiring entrepreneurs often skeptically ask: "Even if contracts and courts may exist, and maybe (sometimes) serve their function, what if I cannot (or do not want to) use the legal system to enforce agreements? In this case, why are Camille and her colleagues so sure that (A) villagers would start up (or expand) businesses and (B) pay what they owed?

How, I further wondered, could this mini-grid (if it got built) be financially viable? Could it make enough money? To satisfy profit-seeking foreign investors? In a village where a filling meal of cakes and coffee for six people at a café (both of which are prepared over a charcoal fire next to a tailor using a hand-powered sewing machine, both pictured at the end of this section) costs (even at possibly inflated prices) less than two US dollars?

5.4. A hand-powered sewing machine in use at a café, in the village of Marosely, Madagascar. (Image by Adam J. Sulkowski.)

5.5. Clockwise from lower left corner: author Adam J. Sulkowski and Raïssa Alaoy, Camille André-Bataille, Eric Klose, and employees of ANKA Madagascar having coffee and cakes at a café, in the village of Marosely, Madagascar. (Image by Adam J. Sulkowski.)

Know your customers and build relationships

Marosely villagers and their leaders independently explained why they trust the people and entities building mini-grids in their village. They said that they appreciated regular consultations and time invested in relationship-building. Iry Raïssa Alaoy (who goes by the name Raïssa) is a Malagasy business development consultant at ANKA who is dedicated to long-term consultations with people in Marosely and other villages. Similarly, Aurélie Buffo of Experts-Solidaires (an NGO that cooperates with ANKA to expand electrification) moved to the region—sometimes living in Marosely for many days at a time—to build relationships. A meeting with villagers and their representatives is pictured at the end of this section.

Raïssa and Aurélie's investment of time in getting to know the needs and wishes of their potential clients has built a consensus around the need for local services and, therefore, the viability of new and expanded small businesses and the ability and desire of locals to pay to keep the electricity flowing. Raïssa added the interesting detail that rural electrification will allow more young people to work and live close to their families, as many would prefer (rather than being forced to migrate to a city).

5.6. A community relations representative meets with villagers and their leaders, in the village of Marosely, Madagascar. (Image by Adam J. Sulkowski.)

Boosting local farms and food processing: why it matters

Raïssa is also accountable for local consultations that are a part of ANKA's Agri-Grid initiative, a part of its Mini-Grid 3.0 approach, which specifically will encourage villagers to make the most of local plants that already grow in their yards that go underutilized, or other resources. She explained: "Although we produce staple crops such as cassava, maize, and sugar cane which could be processed into other commodities such as flour, nutritious products, or sugar, Madagascar is a net *importer* of these kinds of products."

Two Malagasy businesses show that it is possible to profitably process underutilized local plants into higher-value products for both domestic consumption and export. Suzanne Jaouen of Moringa Wave explained that the Moringa plant is seen as nearly useless locally, around village residences, but is prized as a trendy powdered dietary supplement in Europe. Her company hopes to scale-up to both sell more of their product abroad and to educate and distribute more locally to help combat malnutrition. Similarly, Ken Lee Randrianarisoa, founder of Soanamad, turns cassava, breadfruit, and other local vegetation into gluten-free flour and baked goods, including cookies and baguettes.

The only remaining questions involve math and relationships: can all of these entities (including startups engaged in food processing) secure enough financing and then make enough revenue to sustain themselves, allowing them to pay for, among other things, electricity from a local mini-grid?

Tips on entrepreneurship in a tough environment

How do these people keep hope alive when things go badly? Especially in a place famous for nightmarish deforestation? At a time of worldwide environmental collapse? When they see suffering? And when they are very aware that institutions such as courts or other parts of the government can fail?

Aurélie borrowed from an anecdote about a little bird that fought a forest fire by dropping water from its beak: "The other birds laughed at her, but she said, 'I will do what I can.'" She added: "I live in Marosely—I can tell you that already, before the grid is active, there is a difference in people's lives. There is hope and excitement."

Raïssa elaborated on some generalizable lessons: "'Development'—it is such a big and overused word—we sometimes are not sure what it means, and some traditionalists and conservatives can instinctively be against change, so it is not easy. But we see that if we get everyone involved, it is easier. This is not something anyone can do on their own, but working with partners makes things happen. It takes time. Our continuous communication increases the chances that this tool will be used and that its implementation will last." Interestingly (to an outsider), safety and gender roles were never mentioned by these three women as challenges to leading and managing change.

So, did they succeed? Does Marosely have a mini-grid?

By the time Eric and I finished our site visits, the pallets had all been successfully unloaded with no damage. Solar panels and equipment were in the process of being installed. Marosely now has a working solar power installation and mini-grid.

Expect the unexpected, and the impact of the 2020–2021 COVID-19 pandemic

Having an operational mini-grid was not the entirety of the end goal. ANKA was about to start incubating startups, as planned. Even before the COVID-19 pandemic began in 2020, however, it was discovered that rats had chewed through electronics. It took months to secure and replace the needed parts.

Then the global pandemic hit. Madagascar was one of several places in the world where an herbal concoction was first touted as either a preventative treatment or cure for COVID-19. However, eventually, the country was placed under the kind of nationwide lockdown that became familiar to many during the pandemic. Whether ANKA Madagascar succeeds in using mini-grids to power a re-localization of local food economies remains to be seen.

Next steps: sustaining a fragile balance in many ways

ANKA Madagascar's Co-CEO, Nico Livache, added that a key to their success so far has been coordinating "a diversity of funding sources and partners," including:

- Experts-Solidaires, an international NGO providing technical expertise,
- Ground Squirrel Ventures, an impact investment fund (mentioned toward the beginning of this chapter),
- corporate foundations (EDF, Nexans, Synergie Solaire), and
- a financing program of the World Bank.

In Nico's words: "As fragile as the unloading of the panels seemed, so is the balance in development projects—it lies in the ability of all these actors to work together."

Takeaway lessons that could help you in other situations in life and business

(1) The people of ANKA Madagascar and their partners and clients in Madagascar, as well as the other Malagasy entrepreneurs mentioned in this chapter, are all role models of keeping a constructive outlook and mindset. They focus on what could be—what can be done with the resources that they have—and on taking steps in their own realm of influence to create a better future.

(2) Getting to know the pains and goals of potential customers can be essential to imagining a plan for an economically viable operation to meet their needs.

(3) Similarly, taking the time to build relationships of trust can build confidence that a plan will work, even if legal systems cannot be relied upon to enforce commitments.

(4) As noted previously in this book, legacies and more recent history may have resulted in perverse realities, including situations where nutrient-poor imported food is more popular than locally-sourced healthy food. However, these flawed systems may actually present opportunities.

(5) As also noted in other stories in this book (both those of the featured entrepreneurs and my own), it pays to reach out and ask for help—whatever warnings we hear, there are many people who authentically enjoy helping others. Asking for help can even lead to more help than we expect.

Chapter 6

Colombia: Resurrecting Rainforest during a Civil War

I HAD READ and heard about Paolo Lugari's self-sufficient reforestation community, known as Las Gaviotas, since 2005. But its rich history dates back over half a century now. For many years, the UN had flown Lugari to other regions of the world to share his insights and approach. In the 1990s, NPR correspondent Alan Wiesman wrote a book about the village (*Las Gaviotas: A Village to Reinvent the World*).

None other than Colombian novelist Gabriel Garcia Márquez, upon visiting Las Gaviotas, declared Lugari to be the "inventor of the world." Las Gaviotas is a model of a restorative enterprise. Both in Colombia and in the rest of the world, Lugari's approach to thought and action has prompted others to wonder whether economic development can be adjusted so that our activities have constructive side effects rather than harmful ones.

6.1. Paolo Lugari—founder of the reforestation community Las Gaviotas—in his office, in Colombia. (Image by Adam J. Sulkowski.)

A model of success despite civil war and growing climate chaos

We should start with briefly acknowledging context. In addition to decades of infamous and stubbornly persistent armed conflict, severe weather abnormalities have also catastrophically impacted Colombia. The flooding caused by the La Niña Phenomenon of 2010–2011 affected more than 94 percent of Colombian territory. In response to the ensuing destruction of lives, homes, and businesses, the Colombian government established the Climate Adaptation Fund to rebuild infrastructure and construct resiliency projects such as flood defenses. As elsewhere in the world, it is surprising that governmental and private actions on climate have not been a more prominent topic in recent public discourse.

However, most remarkably overlooked in recent coverage of Colombia is the 50th anniversary of the founding of an independent prototype community and the 40th anniversary of its development of an economically viable means of reforestation. This community—Las Gaviotas—and its driving ethos are noteworthy: given the right conditions, its operations and approach to problem-solving could be replicated and scaled-up. Its innovations have long impressed observers, including development specialists, with its potential to impact the future course of life on Earth.

6.2. A collection of innovations devised at the reforestation community Las Gaviotas, in Colombia. (Image by Adam J. Sulkowski.)

Economic activity based on reforestation

Las Gaviotas is a village founded in the late 1960s in the parched grasslands of Eastern Colombia. There, its founder, Paolo Lugari, and other experimenters began planting tropical Caribbean pines. The pines are tough. They can survive in a place too dry for other plants.

Las Gaviotas became famous for showing how much a group of pine trees can help other species to grow. Trees create shade, trap moisture, and alter soil. Other plants then have a fighting chance of surviving. Incredibly, after thousands of years of the area being parched grassland, rainforest seeds dropped in the scat of birds started to germinate and grow. Over time, more and more plant and then animal species that had not been seen in modern times started to thrive.

Pines also produce sap. For decades now, an average population of 200 people has harvested the pine resin on 8,000 hectares, processing and selling it as turpentine, colophony, and rosin for the bows of stringed instruments.

A recent invention by trial and error in the tropics: pine-scented biodiesel

They say smells create the strongest and most durable memories. No wonder, then, that the specific invention from Las Gaviotas that impressed me the most was one that I can smell right now as I write this, long after encountering it. Imagine a distinct yet delightful whiff of the scent of pine. Refreshing. Nice. Got it? Now imagine all existing cars and trucks—the petroleum-powered ones, the ones that poison us with microparticles and gases we can't smell, plus the nasty ones belching visible fumes.

Experiments at Las Gaviotas have led it to develop a biodiesel from pine sap. Until internal combustion engines are taken off the roads, some of them could be powered by the biodiesel developed by Las Gaviotas. To be more precise, Paolo calls the product "energized pine oil." He explained that it is produced through what he called "physical processes, rather than chemical, changing the technological paradigm and resulting in a less polluting variety of biodiesel." I accepted the offer of a ride in a truck powered by the pine diesel. The behavior of the truck was exactly what you'd normally expect. Except . . . that great whiff of pine as it started and drove off.

The pine-scented biodiesel is used on a limited scale. Paolo said anyone is allowed to imitate the technology. But he said production and usage have not spread because of regulations.

Las Gaviotas community members also invented low- or entirely zero-carbon emitting means of providing water, food, energy, and healthcare services. One example is designing buildings that maximize airflow to create free cooling. Another is playground equipment attached to water pumps so that the energy expended in recreational fun pulls water out of a well and into storage for later use. The community's primary side effects are, therefore, carbon capture, rainforest rebirth, and zero-carbon or net-zero carbon emitting inventions.

So, they are sitting on a wealth of patents, right?

No. Paolo has always thought of Las Gaviotas as a playground for experiments and showing what can be done—anyone is free, and very much encouraged, to copy its ideas. He never had the mindset of mainstream American capitalism: to grow, to sell more, and—now that I write this, it sounds awfully militaristic and colonialist—"capture market share." Las Gaviotas sustains itself, and apparently that's good enough for its founder and those who came to live and work there. There's even a waitlist of people that would like to move there. As far as Las Gaviotas's impact on the rest of the world, the goal was always to be a demonstration project—to inspire others to mimic what it does and the thinking and approaches that led to those inventions.

Meeting Paolo, and the power of a brand in a conflict zone

I finally met Paolo in 2018 at his offices for an interview.[1] We spoke about the current state of Las Gaviotas and its potential, given the right conditions, to inspire a wave of prosperous reforestation in Colombia and beyond. Paolo's energy and enthusiasm are still contagious. "Stronger than ever!" is how Paolo would characterize both Las Gaviotas and his drive to keep working, but "Gaviotas is sustaining at its optimum size. It's now a model to inspire other initiatives, and imitation has not happened before because of the armed conflict."

Incredibly, because Paolo and Las Gaviotas were known by all sides of the civil war as purely and quirkily focused on doing something positive with planting and working with their trees, both sides in the intractable civil war left them alone. Not every community enjoyed such an accepted neutral status. In this conflict, as in many, communities were suspected by one side or the other (or both) of harboring sympathizers for the other side. Come to think of it, we can add this to the list of benefits of having a strong brand: even (or maybe especially) in a conflict zone, it's good to be 100 percent clear about your motives, mission, and work (like the Red Cross and Red Crescent) lest someone suspect what you're doing and why. Obviously, there are no guarantees, but apparently a strong brand can help avoid

---

[1] Special thanks to Professor Mónica Ramos Mejía of Pontificia Universidad Javeriana in Bogotá, Colombia for her help in interviewing Paolo Lugari.

problems.

6.3. Paolo Lugari—founder of the reforestation community Las Gaviotas—meeting with author Adam J. Sulkowski, in Colombia. (Image by Mónica Ramos Mejía.)

Now that armed conflict is over, why isn't everyone copying Las Gaviotas?

There are other reforestation projects in the world, but you may also be wondering why more people, communities, and organizations (businesses, governments, charities) are not copying Las Gaviotas. "Why aren't there more villages like this in Colombia? Why not wherever we live? What is the biggest obstacle to imitation?" I asked. Paolo thinks the stumbling block is mindset. He attributed the dominant mindset to the conventional way that startups and investors plan and manage.

"A tropical way of thinking" is needed, according to Paolo.

Echoing other visionaries, he continues to eschew overplanning, dispensing with traditional molds, and preferring to focus on action: "The best way of saying it is doing it—taking a trial and error approach." If they had worked according to conventional guidelines of project management, Paolo said, "no one would have forecasted that Gaviotas was feasible." In other words, a venture with restorative effects (sequestering, by the Gaviotas community's calculations, eighty-nine tons of CO_2 for every one ton of CO_2 emitted) could not have been imagined or deliberately planned, much less realized.

As I write this, I have literally gotten off a call with the heads of a startup and an investor, and Paolo's words have never sounded truer. Even startup founders that want to fundamentally change an industry and create a new market find themselves having to provide forecasts based on the present—meaning existing systems and current market conditions rather than what might potentially be a very different future reality. In Paolo's opinion, this is one reason true breakthroughs are rare. As the quotes in this section illustrate, the Las Gaviotas community created an environment for playful and imaginative experimentation based on what is easily and cheaply available around them. The results have included products like the biodiesel and rosin, jobs, self-sustaining cash flow, an attractive community in which to live, and incredibly, a new and biodiverse forest as a side effect.

"If it exists, it must be possible," and why Paolo stays optimistic

A self-sustaining community that restores the environment may seem far-fetched. But as green business entrepreneur and guru Gunter Pauli has said, speaking about Las Gaviotas: "If it exists, then it must be possible." However, given that so few people have heard of this experimental community, are we to be optimistic about the future? Paolo's response is that "it is criminal to be pessimistic." Just like the rainforest seeds, Colombia's leadership in deploying solutions to the world's climate crisis depends on the right conditions for germination and growth. Environmentally-restorative reforestation solutions such as those proven at Las Gaviotas could be replicated.

Paolo's parting thoughts

I asked Paolo for suggestions on how each of us can start having a corrective impact, given the enormous scale of past and ongoing environmental harm that we collectively have had. "Everyone should get out there and start planting trees—now, and everywhere, and anywhere!"

Takeaway lessons that could help you in other situations in life and business

(1) A regenerative enterprise—that is, an organization that generates more positive side effects than negative side effects—is possible.

(2) As noted elsewhere in this book, a trial and error approach based on playful experimentation rather than careful planning can result in a breakthrough that otherwise has not resulted from conventional approaches.

(3) Innovation can start from simple fundamentals such as planting trees.

(4) A lack of resources and a commitment to finding net-zero emissions solutions, with the right mindset, can lead to

more resourcefulness and creativity and to solutions that may be difficult to imagine in a context of abundance.

(5) Mindset and a strong optimistic brand can be key factors to success—to the point that sworn mortal enemies on two sides of a conflict may (sometimes) both respect your organization and allow it to flourish.

Chapter 7

Kenya: A Counter-Terrorism Officer
Targets Poachers by Listening to Locals

S NAKE BITES. Terrorists. Poaching endangered species. Big data. Photography. Women's entrepreneurship.

These six things don't seem to have much in common, do they? But thanks to the creative thinking and engagement of people on three continents, connections were made that help to predict and thwart profit-driven killing of animals and people. Further, by listening and elevating local voices and visions, more of the context to these issues is being illuminated, contributing to the shaping of conditions in which poaching is less likely to happen. The story in this chapter illustrates a different kind of entrepreneurship, but one with lessons that are generalizable to many contexts, including those involving business.

7.1. Lieutenant Colonel Faye Cuevas with law enforcement officers, in Kenya. (Image courtesy of Faye Cuevas.)

Getting "left of boom"

Lieutenant Colonel Faye Cuevas is a United States Air Force Reserve intelligence officer with over twenty years of experience. She learned four things, among others, from her work on counter-terrorism and counter-insurgency:

    (1) To look for early warning signs and intervene before a

bombing—to get "left of boom."
(2) When enough data is gathered together, unforeseen patterns are illuminated.
(3) Trust and engagement of local people is invaluable.
(4) The black market in animal parts is one of the top four organized crime industries in the world (along with human trafficking, drugs, and arms)—and it is therefore linked to the funding of terrorist groups.

Cuevas was already a decorated combat veteran with experiences in Iraq, Afghanistan, and the Horn of Africa by the time she had a life-changing moment in Kenya. As she described it, she saw an elephant in the wild and realized that, at current rates of poaching deaths, her daughter would not have the same experience by the time she was a young adult. Cuevas became a self-described "accidental conservationist" and explored ways of working with nonprofit conservation groups and Kenyan law enforcement.

Meanwhile, an MBA student gets creative

Meanwhile, Jen, an MBA student in Boston, demonstrated the value of taking an entrepreneurial approach to one's own education. She had a background in conservation work. As an MBA student, Jen was thinking about how to apply lessons from and the resources of the private sector (the corporate world) to the world of conservation and NGOs. Specifically, Jen thought the platform model in tech innovation could be applied, roughly defined as "a means of collecting data from disparate sources to allow others to create matching applications." Faye and Jen spent several months testing their ideas and came up with the initiative eventually known as tenBoma—a name and a concept with local Kenyan roots, as explained later in this chapter.

Interrelated problems

Human–animal conflict (such as farmers being killed by elephants during attempts to defend their crops) creates an enabling environment for poachers. Farmers who are upset with marauding elephants will turn a blind eye or even aid and abet or facilitate the transfer of poached animal parts to the global black market. So, how does one "win hearts and minds" of locals such that they care about conserving animals that they see as dangerous pests?

Ask questions to get at basics—and be ready to walk like a drunkard

A key metaphor used to describe many startup cases is "the drunkard's walk," which uses a comparison to the meandering stumbles of the intoxicated to describe the zigzagging and unforeseeable changes of approach that an entrepreneur sometimes needs to make to get an overall objective accomplished. In this case, Jen spent time researching what were the main causes of death from human–animal conflict. It was snake bites. Of forty-seven deaths in one Kenyan region, thirty-eight were from snake bites—caused by species such as spitting cobras and mambas. This is now recognized as the #1 previously-neglected cause of casualties related to wild animals. So, what better way of winning the loyalty and engagement of local people than distributing snake venom antidotes and helping with snake bite prevention?

Other surprising activities that conservationists now pursue as a tactic for winning the cooperation of local people include: birth control, anti-FGM (or anti-Female Genital Mutilation) campaigns, and women's education. More recently, Faye has been exploring the boosting of local women's entrepreneurship. These are not normally a conservation organization's priorities but are useful in securing local cooperation in local campaigns related to global phenomena like species extinction.

Another unconventional approach for a conservation group was encouraging the use of already-existing, traditional knowledge—beekeeping—to deter elephant encroachment on villages. It should be acknowledged that some frame the overall situation in the world in reverse: that it is arguably expanding human settlements that are encroaching on areas with wild species, not vice versa. Be that as it may, it's interesting that global conservation campaigns find themselves encouraging local populations to use, rather than abandon, native knowledge. Corrupt government officials are another part of the problem of black markets and poaching—this only adds impetus to build trust and incentives for local people to want to cooperate with conservationists.

7.2. Lieutenant Colonel Faye Cuevas meeting with a local matriarch, in Kenya. (Image courtesy of Faye Cuevas.)

Surprising features of the poaching problem: a tsunami of data, but a failure of framing?

According to commonly-cited statistics over the past few years, approximately 100 elephants are killed every day—or about one every fifteen minutes—for their tusks. Conservationists realized that a "fortress model" of protected sanctuaries was failing and that an approach was needed that worked over the broader regions that elephants roamed. Yet the problem of poaching was not being framed in a way that won the attention of local leaders as a priority. At one conference, only three native people went to a session on stopping poaching. The rest went to sessions on trade and business and development.

Besides the failure to frame poaching as an existential threat to locals, several other aspects of the problem may surprise the reader:

- Poverty is NOT the decisive driver of poaching—rather, it's organized crime.
- Competition between conservation organizations may seem inefficient—like dividing a limited total amount of donations—but, while it may create challenges, it may help to force innovation.
- By 2017, there was a "tsunami of data" being gathered about various phenomena (including in rural Kenya), but it was not used for "innovation in intervention."

Ideas that did not work as well as needed

One idea to combat poaching was to concentrate the attention of law enforcement in a problem area. A surge of law enforcement would work—decreasing poaching by, for example, 43 percent. However, it would result in a temporal and spatial shift. In other words, as Faye described, it was like squeezing a water balloon: "You could squeeze and reduce the problem in one place, but it would only move and increase in another."

Another approach was based on sound detection technology. But poachers simply switched approaches, resulting in 70 percent using poison rather than guns to kill animals. Faye and Jen, like others, were realizing that "it's all connected"—one cannot stop poaching if human–animal conflict is not reduced.

"We did not change the game, we gamed the change"

Faye's work in the field of intelligence had conditioned her to look for early warning indicators of imminent attacks. Examining a large enough data set and talking to those in law enforcement revealed: petty theft—of items like tea and sugar—was an early warning indicator of poaching. However, tips to authorities sometimes led to the death of informers. The solution was to set up a system in which tips from locals could be collected and aggregated in such a way that data could be crowdsourced and actionable while protecting the anonymity of tippers.

The name for the initiative was borrowed from a local Kenyan term—"tenBoma"—for the idea that a community can be protected if each member of a community stays aware of what is going on with ten of their neighbors. By extension, locals are asked to stay familiar with an area encompassing ten homes in their vicinity and to notice and report anomalies. This data can be used to help predict what is likely to happen next.

The need to secure the trust and cooperation of locals in tenBoma led conservation groups to further explore activities that were novel for them. These include additional development activities such as securing water access and scholarships and, as mentioned previously, help in the nonviolent protection of crops and steps to avoid and treat snake bites.

Some have said that there was actually a deeper local tradition of stewardship that colonialism had disrupted. Regardless, in the context of the twenty-first century, local farmers in Kenya were quoted as saying, "I thought the wildlife belonged to white people." Consistent with the observations of conservationists in other contexts, it makes a tremendous difference if locals see their interests as aligned with conservation.

Faye believes that tenBoma illustrates what some veteran diplomats have identified as a trend: that aspects of diplomatic functions are increasingly driven by citizen-to-citizen contact and community engagement and cooperation. In other words, rather than the "top-down" approach of a government development agency trying to direct activity, that cooperation more often is happening without a foreign government agency as a middleman or as the source of ideas or know-how. Progress is made, instead, by listening and offering to help with locally-set goals and activities. Some see this as a positive new narrative, or a "bottom-up and beyond" approach.

7.3. Lieutenant Colonel Faye Cuevas meeting with locals, in Kenya. (Image courtesy of Faye Cuevas.)

One example of a "bottom-up" approach: Lensational

Lensational is an example of the companies that Faye advises. As their new CEO, Lydia Wanjiku Kibandi (pictured at the end of this section), explained, Lensational is a young organization that competes with Getty Images and Shutterstock in providing photographs. Their competitive advantage—but also arguably a challenge in competing with big, established incumbent companies—is their social mission: all of the photographs are images created by local women with an intimate knowledge of their context.

Lensational's founder, Bonnie Chiu, was inspired by her grandmother, who used images taken with a camera to communicate, because she was born into a context that did not educate women to be literate. As Bonnie has explained: "I was raised by my grandmother, who, amid conflict and poverty, lost the chance to be educated and still cannot read or write." As Lydia and Faye put it, women are often born into "forced illiteracy" in some places, given that marriage often entails not going to school, if a family can even afford school fees in the first place. Now, because of Lensational, dozens of women who were similarly denied a full education are given opportunities to communicate their realities to the outside world.

As Lydia and Faye explained: "Earned trust is our greatest asset, meaning that clients—whether they are governments, companies, news media, or non-governmental organizations—buy images from Lensational because they know that these are created by local women with a unique, authentic, and better-informed basis for finding and communicating stories." Both Lydia and Faye emphasized: "We were taking on a mission to make the world better, and the sum was going to be bigger than the parts. We often do not look at CVs—we look at sense of purpose and soft skills and team dynamics when deciding whom to hire. Skills can be taught, whereas a sense of mission and interpersonal skills are harder to impart." Faye added: "To this day, I've never seen Lydia's CV."

Yet, after decades working with special forces, widely considered among the most elite "teams of teams" in the world, Faye added a remarkable compliment: "These are, without a doubt, the highest-performing teams with whom I have worked." Lydia added: "Hiring and connecting people with a higher and shared purpose—and seeing how people work together—it was easy to spot a gap and to be proactive in filling it. It is important to emphasize that we hired based on how people worked together and then trained for hard skills."

Faye and Lydia shared a story about the power of the organization's mission to give a platform of empowerment—a specific anecdote about a middle-aged woman who took her first photograph and, in a momentous and emotional experience, said: "This is the first time that I have been able to record a memory." In reflecting on that moment, Faye quoted Steve Jobs's statement that "the most powerful person in the world is the storyteller—the storyteller sets the vision, values, and agenda of an entire generation that is to come." Faye and Lydia recounted how they repeat this truth as a mantra in their ongoing dialogue on WhatsApp. They see on a regular basis the validity of this framing, that "a picture is worth a thousand words, and we have moved from sharing images to visual storytelling. That is the power of the image: it actually holds a thousand stories—and that is where the earned trust is felt and seen."

Lydia added that, in addition to creating a platform to magnify the photographers' power, Lensational is also creating a context in which the photographers feel they can—and are—taking greater control over their lives and are better able to realize their potential. In other words, that Lensational cultivates an awareness within the photographers—that they moved on from being shy, have come into themselves, and have their own answers and opinions." Faye added: "This is such a powerful point—some of these people were never asked for their opinion before, and it showed in early interviews. The impact has been transformational on the people involved."

Lydia concluded: "The bottom-up approach—the value of it—is being recognized and appreciated by clients. It is proof in the marketplace that boosting local voices and diversity and inclusion creates a better service and a better world." A better world, as it turns out, for both the local populations and the natural environment and species that surround them.

7.4. Lydia Wanjiku Kibandi—CEO of Kenyan-based stock photography company Lensational. (Image courtesy of Lensational.)

7.5. Lydia Wanjiku Kibandi—CEO of Kenyan-based stock photography company Lensational—reviewing a digital photo with a local photographer, in Kenya. (Image courtesy of Lensational.)

Takeaway lessons that could help you in other situations in life and business

(1) People from different disciplines, from different realities, and with different lenses can see solutions to wicked problems that might elude a team of specialists in one discipline.

(2) Be ready to question ideological stances and boundaries. For example, people and organizations with the same goals may reasonably disagree on tough questions such as:

- Is it okay to partner with people or institutions in the

military or corporate worlds? With all militaries? With all military contractors? With *all*? Or *none*?

- Is it ever okay to compromise an ideologically-pure position to accomplish a goal—for example, in this context, is it acceptable to entertain the notion of certified non-lethal rhino ranching? This business model does exist. Some conservationists support it because it reduces the demand to poach wild rhinos. To others, it's unacceptable to cut off rhino horns for profit to satisfy demand in other parts of the world.

- Is it useful to occasionally reevaluate what is the "real" industry or mission of your organization and to ask what other activities can help achieve its true long-term aim? Imagine the hesitation of conservation NGOs—to whom donors have given money to save animals—deciding to spend resources on human development and health issues?

(3) Consider taking a holistic approach. In other words, stepping back, seeing the big picture, and "connecting the dots"—maybe there is data that can help you more accurately predict when and where something may happen.

(4) Look for early warnings that may help refocus efforts. Remember: something as simple as considering weather patterns helped improve where to direct efforts. Reports of petty theft were another early indication of criminals on the loose. We'd all love to waste less time and get more results from less effort. So, it's worth investing in the identification of early indications of whether something is worthy of effort or not.

(5) As highlighted in several chapters in this book, it delivers superlative results to hire people based on their sense of

mission and ability to work with others and then train for hard skills.

(6) Consider a platform approach: it may be worth investing time and resources into a standard, single system—like an online database—that allows people to monitor and act upon new information.

(7) User-generated content platforms also help to understand people's motives, their needs, and how to address their needs. Such platforms empower individuals (including the previously marginalized in terms of opportunities) to change reality by sharing their stories.

(8) Progress in conservation, in this context, involved listening to local populations, partnering with them, and supporting their ideas and empowering new local leaders to change their narratives and their reality.

Chapter 8

Cuba: From One Dollar per Day to Top-Rated Place to Stay

I F YOU WANT to see truly innovative entrepreneurship, go where it's illegal. I'm not sure someone has said or written that before. Regardless, that's been one of my favorite go-to lines since visiting Cuba twice and following the journey of a tailor who used to make less than $1 per day. He started, owns, and runs a hospitality business that has regularly been one of the top-rated places to stay in Cuba on Tripadvisor in the years leading up to the pandemic of 2020.

I found Rodolfo by word of mouth (online). He was recommended by a tour guide as an unusual host who took extra care in helping his guests. During my first visit to Cuba, in 2013, I was duly impressed with his network of contacts around the island. If someone was stranded somewhere, no problem—Rodolfo invariably seemed to have "a friend of a friend of a cousin" in the area or passing by.

In 2016, I went back with the primary purpose of interviewing Rodolfo and observing him run Casa Caribe so as to write a case on how to succeed as an entrepreneur in a place where, as a matter of law, the possibility of incorporating a private business does not exist. We ended up discussing whether to co-invest in expanding his business, and I later learned about a way to work around the US embargo—by calling and asking the US Treasury Department if I could break the law.

Rodolfo and I recently caught up and updated this summary of his story—and what later became *our* story.

8.1. Author Adam J. Sulkowski, hostel owner Rodolfo, and Rodolfo's partner, Carlos, standing on a balcony at Rodolfo's hostel, Hostel Casa Caribe, in Havana, Cuba. (Image by Adam J. Sulkowski.)

Identifying the opportunity

Rodolfo was a Cuban tailor earning less than $1 per day. He pined to see the world but could not, due to both lack of resources and Cuba's restrictive travel policies that persisted until 2013.

One way to interact with the world, Rodolfo discovered, was to work in the tourism industry.

The end of the Cold War had led to reforms of the centrally planned Cuban economy. The first reforms to allow earning income from houseguests and other self-employed activities emerged in 1993. The *casas particulares* scheme allows Cubans to host tourists in a private room, house or apartment, bed and breakfast style, for the equivalent of $20 to $25 (in special US-dollar equivalent currency) per night.[1]

A friend told Rodolfo about someone opening a hostel. Rodolfo learned that the policy that permits a bed and breakfast did not place an upward limit on how many persons could be hosted for the night, as long as guests were registered correctly with an immigration office. Rodolfo also learned that the first hostel in Havana was not truly what the international backpacker community expected. There was no common area, book exchange, open kitchen, nor—most importantly—the general spirit and atmosphere where travelers from different parts of the world could meet and share advice and sometimes even team up for onward adventures.

The independent international backpacking traveler is often a budget traveler expecting basic accommodation, such as a bunk in a shared dorm room and shared bathrooms, typically for about $12 to $50 a night, depending on the city in the world and amenities provided. In case you've never stayed in a hostel: sometimes sheets and a towel are included in the price, while other hostels supply these for an extra fee. Breakfast may be included. Policies

---

[1] For information on *casa particulares*, see www.casaparticularcuba.org. There are two currencies in Cuba: the CUP—national pesos for Cuban-to-Cuban transactions—and the CUC, or Cuban Convertible Pesos (pegged to the US dollar) for transactions involving foreigners. When staying at a *casa particular*, one pays in CUC.

and offerings can differ widely as to quiet hours, curfews, dining facilities, and kitchen use. Some hostels offer the option of private rooms with *en suite* bathrooms as well as offering facilities such as swimming pools, rooftop bars, scooter or bicycle rental, massage services, and activity and travel booking.

In short, some hostels are basic and cheap. Some can be "party central" and a horrible choice if you want to sleep. And some can be fancy. Typically, all of them have some greater sense of community than the isolating experience of staying in a hotel. In 2012, Rodolfo secured the rental of a two-bedroom apartment within a block of the seaside in the prestigious and safe Vedado neighborhood of Havana—from someone who trusted that he'd be able to make enough money from running a hostel to cover what was owed.

The motivation to take a creative risk: they say to "start with your 'why?'"

In Rodolfo's own words:

> I want to introduce something I say to my travelers when they ask me why I decided to start hosteling. I use the saying: *"If Muhammad cannot make it to the mountain, then I will bring the mountain to Muhammad [sic]."*[2] I was hungry to know the

---

[2] There are two variations of this saying. The more commonly known (and true to the original) version is: "If the mountain won't come to Muhammad, then Muhammed must go to the mountain." While referring to Muhammad, the Prophet of Islam, the first known appearance is in chapter 12 (Of Boldness) of Francis Bacon's *Essays* (1625): "The people assembled; Mahomet called the hill to come to him, again and again; and when the hill stood still, he was never a whit abashed, but said, 'If the hill will not come to Mahomet, Mahomet will go to the hill.'" Rodolfo's misquotation (intentionally or coincidentally) reflects the essence of what he meant: he wanted to see the world but could not, so he brought the world to Havana.

world. So, I brought the world to my house. If I cannot go to Rome, I bring Romans to my house. If I can't go to Greece, I bring Greeks to my home.

In other words, one of Rodolfo's most important reflections—and a generalizable lesson for entrepreneurs of all kinds—is to take stock of your true motivations. Is it just to make money? Do you actually have a passion for the service or good that you are providing? Is it tied to your intrinsic needs or desires or joys? Would you find the ultimate mission of your activity rewarding if you already had enough money to provide for your household's needs and to assure your comfort?

From watching Rodolfo interact with guests and talk about his experience and future, it is clear that he is driven by a love of guests and a passion for hosting as much as any monetary rewards. This is not to say that research, planning, good execution, and hard work are not essential to success. But a key takeaway is that the answer to the question "would you start a hostel?" (or any other business) should also take into account the answer to the question: "Can you see yourself doing anything else—is this what you most want to be doing, even if you were independently wealthy or, in other words, didn't need the money to survive?"

How to start if you are broke, and how to expand if you lack capital?

During his first four to five months of operation, Rodolfo sold belongings, including family jewelry, to make rent payments. As I will describe later, Rodolfo was always willing to consider new ways to grow and get investments.

Given the choice of what to do with a two-bedroom apartment once you establish (as stated above) that the relevant policy allows for flexibility, would you start a hostel or, instead, a bed and breakfast (limited to one family at a time)?

The quick answer is that a hostel arrangement allows you to host more guests at a lower cost per guest and is likely to be more profitable. In Rodolfo's original location, he had three bunk beds (sleeping six guests) in the same room. At a cost of $12 per bed, he could earn $72 per night. The going rate for a private room in a bed and breakfast with one queen bed would be $25 per night.

Although market rates change, it's still more profitable to accommodate more people in the same amount of space. Other considerations include labor. In hostels, it is often an expectation that guests put the sheets on the bed themselves. In fact, as mentioned above, some hostels charge for sheet and towel rental. There is less labor and lower expectations involved in certain aspects of the guest experience in a hostel. But a successful hostel may also require a greater investment of one's time, energy, and personality, as described next.

How would you go about creating a distinct atmosphere as Rodolfo aspired to provide?

"It starts with the heart," Rodolfo answered. "It starts with what you would like in a foreign country. You would not want it to be unpleasant." He went on to elaborate that he imagines that the worst feeling as a guest is to have a cold and transactional experience or, worse, to feel financially exploited. When pressed for more details on how he succeeds at creating an atmosphere where guests feel at home, mingle, exchange information, and sometimes form groups to pursue onward adventures, Rodolfo explained: "If you don't *make* it happen, it will just be a *casa*. You have to make them feel that this is a home. Make them feel like they have a family here that will take care of them. Generally, owners don't get familiar with their guests."

Rodolfo continued:

> I try to be family far from family. Some guests are traveling six months or more. They have no one with whom to share—they are needing love, someone who is there for them. I try to protect them until the last minute. To get best prices. There are many people who won't care—thinking that foreigners are millionaires. I know [foreigners] have limited budgets. And generally, some hostels in the world do not provide sheets or towels for free. We do, and there's always soap in the bathroom [again, it is not uncommon in hostels around the world to have a "bring your own" approach to everything]. We always welcome guests with a coffee and a cigar, . . . we treat them well.

The hardest obstacle and the weakness it highlighted

Rodolfo worked quickly. The apartment, one block from the seaside in the desirable Vedado neighborhood, opened as Hostel Casa Caribe Havana on January 13, 2013. Rodolfo placed three bunk beds in one room. Sometimes he rented out his private bedroom if guests wanted privacy and their own bathroom or if demand exceeded supply. He set his price at $12 per bunk per night and accommodated an average of six guests per night. Each guest received sheets, a towel, and a breakfast of sliced tropical fruits, fresh buns, and coffee.

Rodolfo relied on the booking website Hostelbookers, operated by a UK company. Hostelbookers was bought by Hostelworld, another booking site, operated by a US company. This is significant, because a small crisis hit when, as an American company, Hostelworld was told that it had to cease listing Cuban options (that previously could be listed on a UK website) because of the US embargo of Cuba. Rodolfo received a letter from Hostelworld politely informing him that it would cease listing his business. Rodolfo had been almost exclusively relying upon this online booking site. Without access to this site, new bookings ceased completely.

What do you do when your source of clients is cut off?

While Rodolfo had created a website, and while there are now at least fifty portals listing places to stay in Cuba, Hostelworld had become such a predominant source of new clients that the scrubbing of Cuban listings practically eliminated new bookings. Overreliance on one source of clients, as this case illustrates, can be very risky.

Rodolfo temporarily came to rely on word of mouth. First, delighted former guests left glowing reviews on Tripadvisor, leading new travelers to seek out his address. Second, Rodolfo gave his guests fliers to take with them to give to other travelers to distribute at their onward destinations. Guests going from Cuba to Mexico, for example, would cross paths with other travelers in hostels and at the airport in Cancun (a popular transit point for getting to Cuba). They passed on the fliers and spread the word that Rodolfo was a good host. Rodolfo said that Tripadvisor and these fliers attracted enough guests to persevere.

One key takeaway is, clearly, not to be overly reliant on one channel for communicating with potential customers. Another is that word of mouth is the base of the marketing pyramid and is especially critical in the hospitality industry. Travelers meet and repeat whether they had a great experience or a bad experience. Rodolfo repeated for emphasis the lesson of this episode: "The world is not as big as we often imagine—the world is not that big." Regardless of the communications channel, whether it is a rating site or a flier passed hand to hand between travelers, this was word of mouth at work, and it illustrates that delighted clients are the best advertising.

How to make it to the top of rankings: a move and relentless work

Rodolfo persevered and gathered input from his clients and tourist guides. The Vedado neighborhood is considered a premium location by locals, but tourists, especially backpackers, appreciate being walking distance to Old Havana's historic sites and museums. This information led Rodolfo to seek a place closer to Old Havana. With the help of a $10,000 loan from an aunt in Florida, Rodolfo bought a flat closer to Old Havana. In local parlance, the new property is called a "house" because it includes rights to a terrace on the roof.

Rodolfo's new location has more rooms, including a ten-bed bunkroom, a private guestroom, and two shared bathrooms in addition to Rodolfo's private room. Another room could be remodeled to accommodate more bunks. The terrace, which features a view of rooftops, a small park, and towers of historic buildings, could be transformed into a bar/breakfast/hangout area. Features of the current space include two small balconies overlooking the street and a common room and dining area with fifteen-foot ceilings and chandeliers.

After one year in the new location, Rodolfo had repaid almost the entire $10,000 loan. His aunt received a part of this amount directly to her bank account through Airbnb deposits. The remainder was brought to her as checks or cash by tour guides and other travelers returning to the United States.

Rodolfo's aunt was able to recoup her loan through collecting Airbnb deposits because of a change to US law. In 2015, the US Department of Treasury authorized the listing of Cuban properties on Airbnb, the popular home-sharing site. Airbnb is proud of its role in the Cuban market. It advertises *casas particulares* on its website and figured out a creative workaround for directing revenue to Cubans advertising property on their website or app.[3] The website further permits linking American bank accounts to the rental of properties in Cuba. Rodolfo's aunt in Florida therefore has listed the current location of Hostel Casa Caribe in Cuba. The site allows her to link reservations so that future guests can make their deposits to her American bank account.

Besides the love and passion that Rodolfo has described in this chapter and moving to a location that was more desirable for his clients, there was one more factor in Rodolfo's success that was on display when I visited him: his work ethic. It was relentless. He was centered on meeting certain nonnegotiable standards for food quality, personally attending to guests, and cleanliness. He even passed on a chance to see a free concert by the Rolling Stones—one of the first mega-concerts on the island—so that he could tend to guests that evening and again in the morning.

Rodolfo's passion, standards, and hard work paid off: by 2016, Hostel Casa Caribe Havana was among the top 10 of over 215 specialty lodgings in Havana (as of 2021: top 15 of 790), as ranked by online reviews posted by former guests. Rodolfo's love

---

[3] Stone, Brad. "Airbnb Is Now Available in Cuba." Bloomberg Businessweek, April 2, 2015. https://www.bloomberg.com/news/articles/2015-04-02/airbnb-is-now-available-in-cuba

of hosting is evident in the reviews visitors have written at the site.

8.2. The common living room of Rodolfo's hostel, Hostel Casa Caribe, in Havana, Cuba. (Image by Adam J. Sulkowski.)

Knowing when enough is enough

Rodolfo grappled with whether to stay and scale-up his business in his current location or to move once again. He showed me an even better location currently for sale. Built around 1900, it is called a colonial building and is even closer to Old Havana sights and a three-minute walk to the sea. It has nine rooms with palatial fifteen-foot ceilings. The property features two courtyards, nine bathrooms, and a sprawling rooftop terrace.

Four rooms around the smaller, more intimate courtyard could be remodeled and marketed as boutique bed and breakfast rooms for $50 per night. The other five could be bunkrooms around the main courtyard. A kitchen, dining room, and hangout area are also adjacent to the larger courtyard. A rooftop bar and restaurant that Beyoncé and Jay-Z have visited is adjacent, while across the street is a restaurant and bar owned by a legendary star of Cuban ballet. The property could be purchased from a family of owners with pre-revolution proof of ownership.

The price of the property Rodolfo was considering was $160,000, half of which Rodolfo could cover by selling all his assets for $80,000. He offered me the opportunity to contribute $80,000 in return for half of the profits and half of the ownership of the property, including the ability to share that stake or receive half of the proceeds in the event of a sale. Having reviewed revenue and cost estimates, the time needed to pay back the original principal could be two years or less. While Cuban courts would almost certainly not enforce the contract, since foreign ownership of property typically requires marrying a Cuban or otherwise becoming a permanent resident, friends and relatives of Cubans in the US do make such investments, based purely on trust.

8.3. A courtyard of a building for sale near Old Havana, in Havana, Cuba, considered by hostel owner Rodolfo as a potential new location for his hostel, Hostel Casa Caribe. (Image by Adam J. Sulkowski.)

"And which law would you like to break, sir?"

The more interesting question than whether to move Hostel Casa Caribe, from my perspective, was whether there was any way around the multiple laws that together comprise the US trade embargo: the roughly half-century-old prohibition under American law of doing any business in Cuba, the quixotic intent of the law being to end Communist rule there. The laugh line of this story involves me phoning the Office of Foreign Asset Control (OFAC) of the US Department of Treasury—the department that enforces such laws and punishes Americans for doing business in countries where we are not allowed to do so. "Hello, Office of Foreign Asset Control, how may I help you?" A voice from central casting asked. A professional, upbeat, Midwest American male's voice.

"I'd like to break the law, please," I stated, doing my best to channel Monty Python's John Cleese (meaning that I was asking for something absurd in a proper-sounding tone).

Without missing a beat, I heard: "And which law would you like to break, sir?" His upbeat, can-do, cheery disposition was unchanged. *God, I love my job*, I remember silently thinking. *Can't wait to repeat this surreal dialogue.*

"So, how do I legally invest in Cuba? I'm asking because someone's suggested it, and also, I'm asking as an academic who's curious and might share the answer with others."

It turns out that one can apply for a special license for free. The review period may take ninety days or more, and the gentleman encouraged me to explain why the investment does not contravene US policy. The cheery fellow explained that the OFAC may then give permission, and, as far as the US government is concerned, you're then "good to go" with your investment in a sanctioned country. Since dozens of countries are under some form of sanctions, this is not an isolated context.

However, independently, both Rodolfo and I decided against making the investment. The critical factor was that Rodolfo and his partner were already burnt out on the relocation and improvements that were necessary to get Casa Caribe to its current state. Another move, the disruption, and the massive scaling of the effort involved would have been profoundly unpleasant, they decided.

A COVID-19 era update

I recently spoke with Rodolfo. The news from Cuba was not good. According to Rodolfo, there is a shortage of food and other goods because "everything is being exported for foreign currency." Ironically, a chain of supermarkets that was kicked out during the revolution is where many Cubans buy essentials, and the store prefers that they pay in US dollars.

Rodolfo's description reminds me of reading about shortages in Cuba in the wake of the collapse of the Soviet Union. Hacks and workarounds are essential for daily survival in a place like Cuba, especially in bad times, like the 1990s and now, in 2020–2021. Rodolfo noted that, ironically, in the parts of the country where the situation is worst—away from the cities—faith in the official system generally seems to be highest.

In discussing this update to Rodolfo's story, we also became aware of a danger and the most important key to the success in many of the stories in this book: a common danger to countries, businesses, and individuals is over-specialization. The pandemic revealed that some countries, including Cuba, had come to be overly reliant on foreign tourists.

Rodolfo understands the importance of another key to success (and to overcoming challenges) that is common across all stories in this book: relationships. He appreciates relationships to such an extent that he is paying employees who have not been able to work because of the pandemic. He moved to Mexico City, where his partner, a doctor, is making comparatively more ($700–800 USD per month). Rodolfo and his partner give some of this money to people traveling to Cuba on humanitarian flights, entrusting them to give the money to his employees. Loyalty and relationships, again, are everything.

An obvious question is why Rodolfo did not wire money to his employees. This is not because of the Cuban government, but because of ours. Between 2016 and 2020 (before the pandemic), the US administration at the time tightened the embargo, cut flights, and stopped Western Union wire transfers, and the restrictions, as of the time of writing this in early 2021, had not yet been lifted.

Takeaway lessons that could help you in other situations in life and business

(1) Start with your passion, then build your activities around it.

(2) Investigate what flexibility might exist within the laws of your location to do more with the same permit—or to possibly even get a permit to do what seems to be barred.

(3) Put your heart into what you do. It can differentiate your service.

(4) Do not become overly reliant on one source of clients.

(5) Word of mouth and a loyal and enthusiastic clientele are the best lifelines in times of disruption.

(6) There is no substitute for a relentless work ethic, attention to detail, high standards, and being willing to sacrifice to put in the time needed to build and improve and deliver your service.

(7) Always be looking for the next opportunity to grow and improve, but be self-aware enough to know when "enough is enough" to avoid burn-out or overextension.

(8) Stay loyal, even when times are bad—relationships within a business and with people outside your business can be indispensable.

Chapter 9

United States: Cooking-Up a Revival in a Former Mill Town

I GREW UP down the street from Hudson, Massachusetts. It's a classic former mill town that once had twelve booming shoe factories. From 1850 until almost 1970, those factory jobs attracted folks from French Canada, Ireland, and Portuguese-speaking parts of the world. Then the factories closed.

Around the time the story in this chapter started, the annual income of Hudson's roughly 15,500 residents averaged to about $35,400. That's 100 times more than the income of many people in places described in other chapters, like Madagascar, Cuba, or Timor-Leste. But given the cost of living in the US, even an hour west of Boston in the semi-rural, semi-suburban woody outskirts of a medium-sized city, towns with such an average income are euphemistically called "working class."

This is not meant to sound nasty, but the phrase "working class" can seem cruelly ironic when applied to a neighborhood with vacant retail space that is conspicuously not filled with the bustle of work. I remember visiting Hudson as a kid and what it was like. Even ten years ago, during the daytime, a lot of nice brick buildings on its main street had empty first floors that were meant to be homes for businesses. After dusk, downtown Hudson was mostly deserted.

The story in this chapter fits the themes of the rest of this book in that a place of seemingly limited resources and disadvantage becomes a context of inspiring innovation. And the story underscores that such contexts are everywhere, maybe even down the street from where you are.

9.1. The main street in downtown Hudson, Massachusetts as it looked prior to the story in this chapter. (Image courtesy of Rail Trail Flatbread Co.)

Want to open your restaurant here?

There are plenty of towns or neighborhoods in the US and elsewhere in the world that, like Hudson, have seen better days. We might live in them, or they might be a few minutes away. If you're like me, when you're in such a place, you pause, take in the sight of the buildings—the craftsmanship, the care that someone put into the brickwork or porticos—and can't help feeling sad to see them empty and not to see more people and activity.

If I share an image in class of Hudson's downtown from a decade ago, students agree the place looks nice. But no one says "yes" when I ask, "So, would you open a restaurant here?" Their explanation is simple: "We'd want to open a business where there is already economic activity going on. And for a restaurant? You want to be where there's foot traffic—a bustling, busy place that is already booming! Ideally? Around rich people!"

"Take this space, we'll work out the lease later."

Karim El-Gamal grew up in Egypt and Canada, came to Boston to pursue further education at Babson College, and there met Michael Kasseris, who grew up with Greek family members in the area running pizza shops. Karim had a nearly lifelong love for pizza and pitched the idea of getting into the business with Michael. "Try it," was Michael's reply. "Work with Uncle Teddy, and if you still want to do this, get back to me." It's hot and hard work, and even dangerous—it turns out you can get injured, even while sharing safety guidance about equipment with new colleagues. But Karim insisted. Somehow, he wanted to have a pizza business.

Another one of Michael's relatives, Uncle Nick, made an offer. Uncle Nick showed Karim and Michael vacant retail space that he owned in downtown Hudson. Nick offered to help them transform the location and to use it. They could make small lease payments at first, and then they would figure out a higher rate later. And Nick offered to help get the place ready for free with his own labor.

Most of my students say they would never accept this offer.

They don't like the idea of uncertain "to be decided later" details, even if the agreement was put into writing—which it was not in Karim and Michael's case. Plus, even if it was an affordable place, the location doesn't seem right: how could anyone make enough money selling anything there, so as to cover other costs like equipment, supplies, and paying employees?

Do your homework

Karim and Michael looked for more information. They asked local people questions. They joined and became active in the Hudson Business Association. They found statistics about the communities around downtown Hudson. A realization emerged: the suburbs around Hudson had a limited number of dining options and no walkable town centers of their own. Some families in surrounding neighborhoods were driving more than thirty minutes away from their home to go out for dinner.

It's important to point out that Karim and Michael had imagined other options. They had even researched whether putting a pizza oven in a delivery van would make sense—to literally deliver it fresh out of an oven. However, this location was more viable than it seemed at first glance.

The power of commitment

Regarding moving to a small and predominantly white former mill town: one might imagine a moment of hesitation or doubt on the part of Karim as to whether an "outsider" would be welcomed in Hudson. But Karim had lived in seven countries and in even more cities, so it was "nothing new to be the new outsider," he said. Karim was the first partner to move to Hudson.

Karim reflected: "I don't need to be anywhere else. By moving here, I sent a huge signal. I'm not an outside investor. I'm here. It's a friendly town. I joined the Hudson Business Association as a business owner. At a certain moment, there was a bit of hesitation only about moving to a small town because I grew up in cosmopolitan places—I thought, *It's going to be small, it's going to be different.*"

Karim admits it was harder to convince his girlfriend to leave her career working in new media in glimmering Dubai to move to a small town in the US. They had both loved living in Dubai and had previously looked forward to being together in a place some consider the crossroads of the world. We'll resolve this personal thread of the story at the conclusion.

Failure was an option . . . or at least a real possibility

One of Karim and Michael's colleagues recalls that Hudson's potential and their business' eventual success was far from an obvious inevitability. He remembers: "The downtown was dilapidated, with broken windows, shuttered fronts. . . . Now it all looks obvious. At the beginning, it did not. They definitely worried. Once we were on the phone with Karim, who was here in Hudson, and he suddenly yells: 'We just saw people running with guns!' And I'm thinking, *Into this town is coming Karim, the international man of mystery.*"

His colleagues joked about coaching Karim on how to fit in smoothly: "Never speak ill of the Red Sox, Patriots, and Bruins [Boston sports teams], and remember, you're from Montreal, but you like the Bruins." They point out some people had problems getting his name right: "He's been called Hakeem, Kamal, Kameel, El-Gamal . . ."

Finally, while a lawyer might strongly advise against an unwritten agreement and nonspecific terms, Karim and Michael do not regret their lease arrangement with Uncle Nick. This is a consistent theme in all the chapters of this book, from Madagascar to Cuba to Hudson: trust in one's business counterparts is everything—a partner or counterpart's trustworthiness and reliability may matter even more than legal formalities. Even in the US, where we think that we're overly litigious and lawyered, Karim and Michael stressed that a lot of their agreements have been and continue to be unwritten. In fact, they said that one supplier (the milkman) "might be insulted and stop doing business" if they were to insist on written documentation of agreements—that it would be a sign of lack of trust or a "slap in the face." The one time they had a well-written contract, "the other side turned out to be crooks, and we lost $15,000." So, in their experience, knowing your business partners is more critical than having a well-written agreement.

An awkward ugly duckling of a place, next to another awkward duckling

Karim and Michael's vision evolved. A lot. They now had a narrow retail space with a dropped ceiling: what to do with it? A pizza takeout counter seemed like a solution. But the location had other problems. It was such a narrow space that getting to the restroom in the back would require walking through the kitchen. This led them to consider whether to possibly lease the adjacent space too.

The problem with the adjoining area was that it was also awkwardly narrow and long, and its floor height was several inches higher than their first leased area. However, the use of this adjacent space would greatly expand the size of the eatery, opening up the potential of including seating areas and room for a bar.

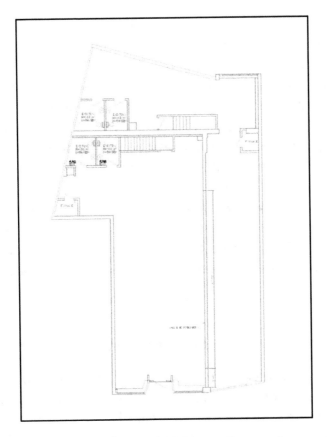

9.2. The original floor plan of the retail space that would eventually become Karim El-Gamal and Michael Kasseris's restaurant, Rail Trail Flatbread Co., in Hudson, Massachusetts. (Image courtesy of Rail Trail Flatbread Co.)

"Holy s**t, are we doing full service?"

The question of how to use the awkward physical space was connected to the core question of what kind of business Karim and Michael planned to run. They considered many ideas, including abandoning the idea of a low-cost takeout counter and instead creating a restaurant. One option included serving scratch-made food made with locally-sourced ingredients. In terms of quality and price, they could consider offering higher-quality menu options featuring new flavors and ideas. Yet they were also mindful that their target market was working and middle-class families still feeling economic uncertainty in 2011. They wanted to keep the price of a meal for a family of four to $30–40.

They were also torn between wanting to offer conventional American comfort food and the possibility of offering novel cuisine. They also considered offering a menu of quality local craft beers at the bar, yet they wanted to maintain an atmosphere where families could feel comfortable. In sum, reconsidering how to use the awkward space led to reconsidering their format, which led to a huge new variety of choices about multiple aspects of menu offerings.

Who was that mysterious random Russian man?

One idea, in particular, captivated the imagination of the partners (once they started imagining a sit-down eatery): having a wood-fired flatbread oven. The oven had the potential to create a charming atmosphere for the expanded seating area. But no manufactured or secondhand option existed to purchase exactly the kind of wood-fired pizza oven that the partners imagined. They wanted an oven that would create an ambiance in the immediate seating area. This entailed certain specifications related to the size of the oven's door and its height above the floor. Further, every customized solution that they explored would be too costly.

Thinking back on their Babson days, Karim and Michael re-called their trip to the Las Vegas Pizza Expo that their professors had encouraged them to attend. Michael recalled sitting next to a man who leaned over and told him in a Russian accent, "I am from Ottawa. I make custom-built wood-fired pizza ovens." Michael mused: what are the chances that a completely random, out-of-the-blue, isolated self-introduction could lead to something valuable? All he had as a lead were those three facts (a Russian in Ottawa who makes pizza ovens)—was it worth his time sleuthing and searching for him online, to get an estimate on the cost of building a customized oven?

These ideas represented zany departures from original plans and a host of new issues. Besides questions of how to physically arrange the large space and construct or purchase equipment and fixtures, human resources would now be a significant challenge. A talented chef would be needed, as well as someone to curate and run the bar. At the time, there was no large local talent pool of chefs, kitchen workforce, and waitstaff needed for this type of venture. So, the business partners would have to consider various options, including attracting talent from elsewhere or possibly training people—a "scratch-made staff" in addition to making scratch-made food. And that might mean hiring people who had no preexisting skills or training or who had possibly made mistakes in life and were starting over.

At this point in the story, Karim and Michael had not opened the business. They were in the midst of months of renovations. They did not yet imagine their precise roles in their own organization once it started operating. The deadline for finishing renovations had passed and been extended several times. One of the reasons for the delays was their ongoing willingness to entertain new options and possibilities as they emerged.

A massive, fundamental change to the plan: "We took a sledgehammer to it."

It is often said that plans are obsolete the moment that they are put into effect. Entrepreneurs change plans continuously to optimally take advantage of serendipitous discoveries and unforeseen opportunities. At first, Karim and Michael planned a fast, casual counter service. Their ideas evolved radically: "It was more like we took a sledgehammer to our original plan, not a pickaxe."

Michael recalls the first moment where he realized they would massively change their plan on the fly: it was during construction—when they decided to double their physical space from 2,000 to 4,000 square feet. As he sketched out and described, they thought that their business would be half the space they ended up using.

Incredibly, as described above, the business as it is today—that it is a destination for dining and not a takeout counter—was based on the awkward location of the restrooms. Karim and Michael's coupling of the two narrow and awkward adjacent spaces also explains their choice to have an open hallway next to an open kitchen, allowing people to not have to walk through the kitchen to access the restrooms. Most remarkably, the height difference between the two spaces turned out to be an asset: they now serve as tiers that offer guests on both levels a view of the open kitchen and the glowing pizza oven.

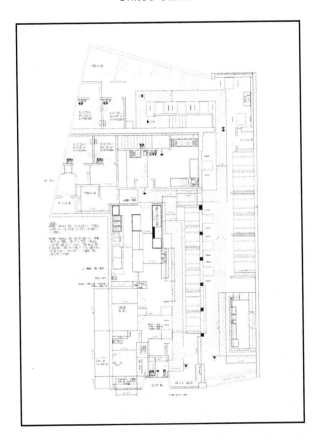

9.3. The current floor plan of Karim El-Gamal and Michael Kasseris's restaurant, Rail Trail Flatbread Co., in Hudson, Massachusetts. (Image courtesy of Rail Trail Flatbread Co.)

The defining sensory focal point was not planned and resulted from chance

When visiting the restaurant, Michael suggests sitting at a booth across from the oven to feel the warmth and see the immediate surroundings partially illuminated by the wood-fire inside. The placement of the fire's opening to create these effects was intentional. It adds to the atmosphere tremendously. Yet this primal, campfire-like ambiance was not part of Karim and Michael's original vision—it flowed, again, from the awkward location of the restrooms and abandonment of the takeout counter concept in favor of an open kitchen and two-tiered seating arrangement.

The design and construction of the pizza oven is another illustration of the role of serendipity and the value of networking. When they realized that they wanted to custom-design and build their own flatbread oven, the partners were disappointed to learn that no one could build an oven for less than $50,000. Michael managed to find the mysterious, random Russian man from the Las Vegas event, and Karim and Michael hired his apprentice to custom design and build the oven. The partners and the apprentice combined two styles into a novel oven with the opening at eye-level to guests sitting in booths across from it.

The oven is now a focal point of activity of the restaurant both visually and in terms of creating dishes. But it was random chance that the wood-fired oven builder decided to share two details about himself at a pizza expo, which the partners had decided to attend at the last minute on the advice of professors. Michael pointed out, while sitting at the booth across from the oven, "Note that when you enter an eatery that is well-designed, the client walking in should always see, in order: (A) something to drink and then (B) food." Ergo the placement of the bar and the layout with the kitchen and oven being the next things that one sees when entering.

9.4. The wood-burning oven at Karim El-Gamal and Michael Kasseris's restaurant, Rail Trail Flatbread Co., in Hudson, Massachusetts. (Image courtesy of Rail Trail Flatbread Co.)

Disadvantages can be advantages

Adapting to small idiosyncrasies played a recurring role in other adjustments. Michael's Uncle Nick—a colorful personality described as "this older guy off the boat from Greece [who is] stubborn, like[s] challenges, [and is] a great carpenter"— recognized and urged two of these unforeseen modifications.

First, that the floor under the heavy new oven would need rein-forcement. Second, he suggested carefully removing the dropped ceiling. It turns out that there was beautiful and ornate tin ceiling concealed above it.

Disadvantages of the location were turned into advantages: the removal of the dropped ceiling, the different, long, narrow strips of space at two different levels, the restroom access issue, and deciding to put an open kitchen in front and parallel to the seating. As the space evolved, in all of these instances, the partners found ways to capitalize on what first looked like prob-lems. Some of the layout was worked out with cardboard cutout model pieces that could be moved around like a puzzle.

"It's yours for free, but you have to get it out"

The story of how Karim and Michael found furnishings and equipment bears mentioning because it illustrates how the part-ners creatively minimized costs. As Karim explained, "We found it all at auction . . . almost every piece of equipment. It was out of necessity plus following the example of Michael's relatives. . . . You can find a good table for $20–100. But sometimes buying equipment at auction—or even for free, if someone's going out of business—means you are responsible for removing the items, meaning you may need to open windows to pivot booths out, . . . 200-pound booths. You might get bar equipment for $2,000–3,000 but may need eight hours to remove it."

How to get top talent to take a risk with you

This vignette is worth sharing because it illustrates again the role of serendipity and sharing one's vision and how a creative tension and diversity of styles can lead to an eventual unforeseen out-come that is "greater than the sum of its parts." The identification and recruitment of a top-quality chef fundamentally altered what Rail Trail Flatbread—the name of Karim and Michael's restaurant—eventually became. As the partners explained: "How did we find Tom? Originally, we were looking for a friend or expert in the culinary arts to review and vet the menu. Tom came with stripes—he's even mentioned in a tell-all book [about the best kitchens in Boston] . . . as an ambitious young cook called "Kenny," . . . he was working at the top level of kitchens. But we thought: 'if he sees this potential beauty, and sees the building, and knows there is an open head chef position, . . . he may want to stay.'"

The partners elaborated: "Tom is from upstate New York—a town of 2,000—the kind of place where people are born and then die there, 'from baptism to death.' So, we saw the chance that he might like Hudson. We delicately romanced him to join the team. On the ride out, we deliberately took back roads. We just hit it off. We discussed all the taboo topics: politics, religion, love, music. Eventually, he said, 'I would love to work for you guys, but I need to make a change to the food we'd be serving.'" Tom had suggested the style for which Rail Trail has become famous and praised: "casual, quick, American fare, made in a gourmet manner," as the partners call it, "like duck on a flatbread . . . or with smoked Spanish octopus."

The partners described an interesting creative tension with Tom that they partially attribute to their different backgrounds:

Tom wanted "nice stuff," and we kept saying, "Get your mind out of Cambridge and Boston, . . . no, . . . we want it really casual." Tom loves junk food, . . . but he turns it into something fancy. Like a chicken patty sandwich, but he'll make it a Thai chicken patty . . . with fresh herbs, fish sauce, . . . fifteen steps, . . . and on buns that we cooked. He is talented and hard-working but not a planner. He's an instinctual person. Apparently, Tom knew on a deeper level that things would work out. He is a "visceral-gut-feeler-type." . . . On a gut-level, he felt an instinctual "yes."

In contrast, Michael said: "Karim is more strategic, playing out all options. . . . He thinks-through and deliberates. Tom doesn't do that, he's more of a 'feeler.'"

Another moment of pivoting to a new concept was the partners accepting the idea (from friends who consulted with bars) of having a beer selection and then abandoning the idea of offering just three well-known beers. They ultimately accepted the advice to have a curated selection, deciding to be full-service and higher quality, offering twenty craft beers.

9.5. Food served at Karim El-Gamal and Michael Kasseris's restaurant, Rail Trail Flatbread Co., in Hudson, Massachusetts. (Image courtesy of Rail Trail Flatbread Co.)

Seeing the business from the customer perspective

While refining their opportunity and thinking-through potential business models, Karim and Michael kept their target customers in mind. They also stayed within their passion and strength—pizza (or, as they would later call it, "flatbread"). There are many choices restaurants can make to manage sales and costs. One option is to limit the range of menu choices—"make your own flatbread" but with "minimal options." The owners found that in their uncle's previous pizza business, customers were given numerous options but seldom actually customized their pizzas. So, they decided to go with a less-is-more approach.

This is based on the principle of the "Paradox of Choice"—people are more satisfied with fewer options. Fewer options also makes material planning and sourcing easier to manage. It is also important to consider how the decision to source locally would affect the menu item choices. Karim and Michael decided to leverage local sourcing to change the menu every few months. Karim described their supply chain and operations as something of an ad hoc (flexible, relying on contacts) approach to local sourcing: someone scouts and sometimes buys large amounts of something because it's available, and then they figure out what to do with it.

Recap: so much progress . . . but not open, and not a cent in sales

To summarize Karim and Michael's progress so far: over the course of 2012, the partners committed to a sit-down restaurant featuring locally-sourced food, including flatbreads. The remodeled restaurant space included a two-tiered seating area with a bar on the upper level and an open kitchen on the lower level. An apprentice of the "mystery pizza oven maker" from Ottawa constructed a customized pizza oven that was to be the visual and operational focal point of the restaurant, creating a warm ambiance. They were successful in wooing a sous-chef from a top brand restaurant in Boston, who worked with them on "classing-up" American comfort food and hired employees from the local population.

As of December 2012, however, the partners were nearly broke and had delayed opening several times, to the point it was almost a running joke in the community. The physical space was just about ready to accept and serve guests, but just barely.

"Broke, and a joke"—do we open before we're ready?

As Karim and Michael explained: "We were so broke—we could not afford any more waiting—we were months overdue with construction . . . and a joke downtown. . . . It became a joke to ask, 'When will it open?' We were on edge all the time, [asking ourselves,] . . . 'Is this the right decision' [regarding several questions]." They were also asking themselves: "Every day we are not open, how much does it cost?"

On December 5, 2012, they had a "soft opening" for family and friends. The partners recall that there was still "cardboard and butcher paper on the windows. . . . Anybody here . . . was still sweeping and polishing." The soft opening allowed them to catch and resolve glitches before opening to the general public. They decided "We're ready enough," and opening night was set for December 12, 2012 (12/12/12). That night, they were still training people and had no money to pay anyone, yet had twenty people waiting outside their door to try the new restaurant in town.

Wait, what about marketing?

The partners decided on "no normal media. . . . We focused on naturally growing our network on social media—getting to 3,000 or 4,000 followers (the maximum that a public relations firm thought they would get)." They later quickly grew to 6,000 online followers. "You can almost pay for likes, . . . but ours are organic, . . . our followers sought us." This was something Jason, who was joining Karim and Michael as their third partner (as described later), "was excited to do. . . . He said, 'Gimme access' and started posting online. Karim's wife and Jason built momentum [on social media]."

The partners have continued a no-advertising policy, preferring to engage in local sponsorships of charitable and other good causes. Because no dollars go into advertising, they have resources to "support local education, arts, . . . charities, . . . [and] sports. . . . We have a policy that we will sponsor anyone with a local cause. We learned about this at the pizza expo. We give donations to local charities in the form of gift cards worth $33— so it is easy to track them back, . . . any request from a 501(c)3 [nonprofit organization], . . . a local baseball team [for example], . . . we want them to eat here. . . . We are a community-based business." As illustrated in a later section of this chapter, this use of marketing dollars exclusively for supporting local charities paid surprising dividends.

Growth, rebellion, toxic employees (that seem indispensable)—and what next?

Within months of opening, the following issues arose. First, the two founding partners were stretched to a breaking point, starting their days early in the morning and working past midnight into early the next day. There were a couple of potential solutions.

One possibility was to invite a childhood friend of Michael's, Jason, who had industry experience, to be third partner. Another was to hire a manager to help with the responsibilities.

The second issue that arose involved problems among the staff. Some of the employees had made mistakes earlier in life, related to substance abuse and criminal behavior, and their old habits were hard to kill. Other employees hurt morale and were disrespectful to the partners, gossiping and infecting others with bad attitudes. And third, while customers were happy with the food and drink offerings, some had asked about dessert options as Rail Trail did not offer many desserts. While the atmosphere of the downtown was gradually improving, there were still vacant retail spaces, including one across the street.

Stretching themselves to breaking point and "cancerous" employees

A small number of people can spread an infectious bad attitude and negatively affect everyone in the organization. Karim and Michael offered these quotes to imagine the context of the crisis: "Our head bartender disappears, . . . we had cooks with mental meltdowns, . . . former druggies, . . . someone had expected '$13 an hour to cook. . . . But this is different, . . . we're working our ass off!' Another employee declared, 'This sucks.' Our response was: 'Then go! I'll do it!'" The partners also offered these quotes to elaborate on how many hours they were working: "At midnight, we closed and started making bread for the next day. . . . So, we were working until 3 a.m. the next day. We did whatever was required. . . . That's how we all ended up sleeping across the street."

It seems like it would have been difficult to imagine systems even if the partners had tried: "We were not talking operations,

. . . suppliers, employing, and stress-testing equipment. . . . Something might not have been hot enough, . . . something else was getting clogged. . . . At 7 a.m., we would realize a plumber was needed. Twelve midnight would come . . . and the question would be 'now what do we fix?!'"

They said it is difficult to convey how chaotic things were, between the problematic employees and not having everything systematized: "We had a 110-seat facility with no sections. . . . The waitstaff was cutting its own sections, . . . we were pooling tips, . . . and the problems of cancerous employees started—we heard, 'We're not coming in unless you give us a raise.' This was when we were relying on everyone to help out. . . . We were still in the mode of 'let me show you how to do this.'"

Hire so that you can fire

So, what do you do with unruly or insubordinate or sabotaging or cancerous employees? Karim, Michael, and Jason (plus uncle Nick) decided to be aggressive with hiring and firing when it became clear that some employees were a cancer. They reached "a point of realizing we will do this on our own if need be, but we will take back ownership." They elaborated: "Anyone who attacks company culture is a cancer—whether it is harassing other employees, intimidation, disobeying, tardiness . . ."

They continued:

It became a question of "how much do we put up with?" We decided we must gain momentum in hiring—to have enough people that we could easily fire the people who infected others with bad attitudes. We have created a culture now, . . . but there were a lot of s**theads in the beginning, . . . for example, a server with an active campaign against how we were doing things, hinting that she may leave. And this was our best server—she could sell anything, but she was cancerous, terrible for our culture. . . . And we were asking, "When can we move on, when do we cut bait?" We had other tough employee situations—a drug addict that lets you down, formerly on heroin. We may have had a 50/50 ratio of better vs. worse staff. Some were great. But we had to become more selective. We had to aggressively hire so that we could fire.

The partners had to directly involve themselves with all the staff issues. They added: "Tom is a great chef, but he's not into management—he's a worker octopus."

Never too early to plan operations and an oversupply of employees

It turns out that figuring out standard, repeatable operating procedures for a business *after* it opens is a common mistake for entrepreneurs. It might be easier said than done—one of those theoretical "academic" things about "how it ought to be" that just doesn't work in reality. But Karim and Michael's story illustrates that maybe some pain could be avoided by planning operations and "over-recruiting" talent so that no employees feel indispensable and at liberty to turn rebellious.

How to add a partner to the ownership and management

Once Karim and Michael decided that Jason could add value to the operation, much as with the initial question of whether to accept the offer to lease the location, most attorneys would advise agreeing upon specifics in a written agreement. Again, this case is arguably "an exception that proves the rule." The three agreed to try out working together for several months before agreeing that they would put down an agreement in writing.

The three chose to form an LLC and agreed upon a detailed partnership agreement. The partnership agreement contains provisions on how decisions are to be made and succession contingencies. The LLC is a good choice given the specifics of their case: it is quickly formed, limits the owners' liability to the value of their investments, and allows distribution of profits to the owners being taxed just once as personal income (rather than the business form being taxed first, as is the case with a C corporation).

Being a hometown hero may help you with your legal rights

Rail Trail, by attracting foot traffic to downtown Hudson, encouraged other entrepreneurs and investors to take a risk and open businesses. By living in Hudson, helping to revitalize the downtown, and deploying their marketing dollars into sponsorship of local charities, Karim and Michael garnered a tremendous amount of goodwill. They also doubled down on their local bet by not expanding beyond Hudson. Instead, the LLC formed by Karim, Michael, and Jason leased a vacant space across the street and opened an ice creamery.

Almost immediately after Rail Trail opened, the partners had started researching ice cream shops. They knew they wanted a wide variety of options, with as many locally-sourced ingredients as possible. Beyond that, they believe New City Microcreamery is the first in the world to make large batches using liquid nitrogen, which creates smaller crystals, resulting in a smoother taste.

When an additional liquor license became available, the local committee passed over a proposal from a large chain restaurant and awarded it to the three partners. The partners used it to open a speakeasy—an unadvertised bar behind an unmarked door at the back of their ice creamery. Their story therefore illustrates that generating goodwill in a community can directly lead to winning a legal right that they otherwise may not have enjoyed.

Hudson: a dining destination—who would have foreseen that?

As mentioned early in this story, most students declare that they would *never* consider pursuing the initial opportunity that Uncle Nick offered to Karim and Michael. Yet, despite all the risks, Rail Trail now attracts diners from Hudson, surrounding towns, and even Boston and beyond. It also earns top reviews from gourmands. The reputation of Rail Trail is such that guests have been known to come and wait two hours to be seated on weekend evenings. Likewise, the partners' New City Creamery and "<>" speakeasy (pronounced and sometimes written as "Less Than Greater Than"), situated across the street, are popular and profitable businesses with their own fan base.

The business partners stumbled upon, with the ice cream shop and speakeasy, an ingenious solution to one of the toughest challenges of popular dining locations: if the atmosphere is *too* nice, guests don't want to leave. But from the business perspective, an owner wants to make room for the next guests that are hopefully waiting outside. So, offering the option of dessert across the street means guests have that option and an attractive reason to get up after finishing their meal, giving the Rail Trail staff the chance to prep for and seat the next guests—a win–win.

The latest

The three partners eventually opened a second New City Creamery location in Cambridge, Massachusetts. In total, their four operations now employ 140 people. And, to resolve the personal thread from the start of the story, Karim convinced his then girlfriend, Lora Markova, to move from Dubai with a marriage proposal. Lora is now co-owner of a yoga studio in Hudson. Karim was a founding member and is now Vice President of the Hudson Business Improvement District, the first of its kind in Central Massachusetts. The District uses a small tax on property to pay for an art festival, sidewalk dining, and a central website promoting Hudson's downtown—that same downtown described at the start of this chapter was referred to by a regional business journal in 2020 as a "star of MetroWest."

What gets them excited now?

In several conversations in recent years—when he visits classes or even in casual catch-up chats—Karim evangelizes about the power of an open-book management approach, meaning teaching financial literacy and sharing accounting information and profits with all employees. "It's incredible what they'll see: we built this business, but if they realize the impact on our bottom line and see how things work and know they have something to gain, then someone cleaning-up the kitchen or prepping food before the evening's start—really, anyone—might see something we missed. Maybe it's something wasted here or duplicated there. And those little details of how we can run better add up and make a big difference."

Karim added one more memorable reflection: "Also, it's funny: many of our employees say, 'Oh, I thought you made more'—so, it's actually good for morale for everyone to see that we're not taking some kind of obscene amount of profits home with us. If they don't see the numbers, some may really think it's millions of dollars we're taking from the business, and they wouldn't guess how much is reinvested back into it."

Takeaway lessons that could help you in other situations in life and business

(1) Start with—and maintain—a core activity related to something you love, but be willing to embrace "the drunkard's walk" or "pivoting," meaning adjusting to fresh information and opportunities and even changing the goal or strategy.

(2) Some solutions may not fit the textbook version of the ideal way of doing something; within reason, be open to putting trust in close friends and family.

(3) Some opportunities look doubtful at first, until more information is gathered.

(4) Be open to seeing shortcomings—with the right adjustments—as opportunities to differentiate and find value.

(5) Attract talent by sharing your vision and giving people the chance to exercise creativity, take ownership, and see the chance to create something exciting and new.

(6) A "soft open" or testing a less than perfect "version 1.0"— and then refining a product or service with each iteration— is not just for software or technology companies.

(7) Avoid having indispensable employees—this may include people near the top of the organization. Instead, develop systems early and be ready to let go and replace people that negatively impact culture.

(8) Showing commitment to a community and helping it develop can win the trust and loyalty of local decision-makers, which can contribute to a favorable permitting decision. In

fact, supporting your community can be better than conventional advertising.

(9) Educate and share information about your business, including your financials—anyone in your organization may see opportunities to improve how things are done, which could have a positive impact.

Chapter 10

Suriname: Preserving the Maroon Culture and Rainforest in a Pandemic

O N THE NORTHEAST SHORES of South America are two countries and a territory that are neither majority Spanish- or Portuguese-speaking (like the rest of the continent). These are the sometimes overlooked "Guyanas," as they are often called. One of them is a former Dutch colony: Suriname, a country of less than 600,000 citizens located between formerly British Guyana (now Guyana) and French Guyana (still a part of France). The population is concentrated mostly in the capital on the coast. Most of the Guyanas, including Suriname, are covered in relatively intact rainforest.

10.1. A rainforest and river, on the outskirts of the village of Jaw Jaw, Suriname. (Image by Adam J. Sulkowski.)

Meet Ma' Bele

Ma' Bele was born in Suriname but studied and worked in the Netherlands between the ages of nineteen and thirty-five, returning home six years ago to a Maroon village in the jungle, far from the coast, where he started and has run a different business from what he expected. He returned with his Dutch wife and child because he felt deeply attached to his home village. However, staying in Jaw Jaw (pronounced "Yee-ow Yee-ow") has come at a great personal cost.

One of Ma' Bele's wishes in life was to be a present and involved father—something he lacked in childhood. Yet his wife missed her family and moved back to the Netherlands with their daughter. While on good terms with them both, and though he communicates with his daughter daily, his calling to stay and contribute to the evolution and understanding of his place of origin has meant a profound sacrifice.

10.2. Ma' Bele holding a Jaw Jaw visitor's child, in the village of Jaw Jaw, Suriname. (Image by Adam J. Sulkowski.)

How and why we met

By early 2020, I had become comfortable telling folks about my habit of collecting stories and accustomed to people pointing out or introducing me to remarkable individuals. And so it happened in Paramaribo, the capital of Suriname. I was strongly encouraged to take a bus and then a trip by motorized longboat up a river into the rainforest to visit a village and stay with Ma' Bele. I expected to learn about his opinions and that of others in the area—about whether tourism is compatible with preservation of their culture and natural environment. We discussed both those issues, as well as more generalizable observations for people anywhere.

Who are the Maroon?

The villages of people known as the Maroon were founded by African slaves who escaped Dutch colonialists and established communities in the jungle along rivers in present-day Suriname, in this infrequently visited corner of South America. The former location of Jaw Jaw was flooded when a dam was built in the 1960s to generate power for the bauxite industry (a part of the supply chain for aluminum). About twenty Maroon villages were relocated. Jaw Jaw was one of them. Therefore, the location of Jaw Jaw where Ma' Bele grew up is not the same as where his parents and grandparents lived. This particular context begs questions about what it means to be rooted in a location, or what it means to be attached to a place or identity or community, or what it means to be authentically local. Ma' Bele's journey running his business is arguably a living meditation on these questions, in addition to holding some generalizable lessons.

Suriname negotiated full independence in 1975 and subsequently experienced internal armed conflict in the 1980s. Regardless of the country's travails, for decades, the Maroons have fascinated outsiders, prompting curious foreigners to travel to lodges upriver and stay in close enough proximity to go on day-visits to walk through and see Maroon village life, even if just for a few hours.

From chickens to check-ins

Ma' Bele first attempted to run a chicken farm. It turned out not to be as lucrative as he expected. Meanwhile, he noticed that tourists staying at river lodges would go on guided day-walks through his village of about 350 people and pause near his home. He asked why and found out that they were intrigued by the village and wished they could stay longer rather than going back to their river lodges on islands away from the village.

So, Ma' Bele planted almond trees for shade, built a nice picnic area, and then built one hut in a traditional style and then another, until he now has four with a capacity for up to ten guests for whom he cooks and shows around and arranges activities with friends. The activities include swimming, fishing for piranhas (yes, in the same river as the swimming), and going on walks through the jungle to areas where villagers grow and process a significant part, if not a majority, of their daily food needs.

Ma' Bele relied upon word of mouth from happy guests to grow his stream of clientele, and he has no intention of building more capacity. Instead, he is finding satisfaction in four goals:

(1) being an attentive host,
(2) contributing to the local school and tutoring students every night in computer skills and geography,
(3) eventually building a museum about Jaw Jaw, and
(4) building a house for his use in old age.

10.3. A path and dwellings at nighttime, built in a traditional style, in the village of Jaw Jaw, Suriname. (Image by Adam J. Sulkowski.)

10.4. Ma' Bele tutoring students at computers, in the village of Jaw Jaw, Suriname. (Image by Adam J. Sulkowski.)

Troubles (even in paradise) and how to surmount them

Ma' Bele has experienced two generalizable difficulties anyone may confront, and he shared his ways of dealing with them. First, there is the problem client—or, more specifically in this case, the arrogant and condescending clients who have asked, "How could you give up life in a city to live here in the jungle?" I was authentically shocked to hear this—more so that someone could not see the appeal of fresh air, lush surroundings, local fresh and healthy food, and no office-related stress on the banks of a swimmable river than that someone could lack the tact of keeping such a lack of appreciation to themselves. Bele mused: "What can you do? There are guests that take energy and those that give you energy. Do you waste energy or try to quickly let it go and let them leave with their silliness?"

The next difficulty Ma' Bele has experienced is a recurring theme that arose: "The work ethic is different here." I pushed Bele several times for an answer to how he approached this challenge, because, regardless of whether it is rooted in cultural differences or divergent personal standards, most of us eventually experience the problem of working with others who may have an irritatingly different approach. Echoing a theme heard elsewhere in this collection, Ma' Bele started by saying: "Working with others is everything. Especially in a village. In a city, you are a number. In a village, you need to work with everyone."

Bele elaborated: "First, you cannot come in and act like you are more important than everyone and tell them what to do. You have to work as much as you want others to work. The other thing is to pay at the end of a job being completed rather than [paying] a wage or salary. Finally, adjust expectations: 'Something may not be done today, but it will be done tomorrow.'"

Is tourism changing the culture? Is tourism ruining the environment?

With regard to the first question, Ma' Bele said, "Maroon culture is changing anyway and will change. That is inevitable. It is just a question of how. And the young people should understand and work with the outside world, to have a choice of moving to the city or elsewhere or staying here." And yet traditions are maintained, such as cassava straining and bread-making (pictured at the end of this section).

The answer to the second question is based on broader context that Bele and others shared and which can be read about elsewhere. In short, because Maroon villages generally attract a small number of visitors genuinely interested in better understanding a different culture, the region is not yet suffering the kind of environmental trashing caused by the ravages of mass tourism as practiced and experienced elsewhere.

10.5. Straining cassavas to make flour, near the village of Jaw Jaw, Suriname. (Image by Adam J. Sulkowski.)

10.6. Cassava flatbread cooking, in the village of Jaw Jaw, Suriname. (Image by Adam J. Sulkowski.)

Community forestry: what a Nobel Prize, the Maroon, and saving the world have in common

The next obvious question to a visitor to Jaw Jaw is how much the Maroon's own slash-and-burn agriculture, logging, and hunting impacts the jungle. By their own account—including that of the veteran logger with whom I spoke—villagers state that they have an interest in preserving what the environment provides for their grandchildren. This interest prompts them to set limits on what and when they kill (for example, not taking pregnant animals) and rotating crop areas within designated territory after two to three years so that the forest and soil can regenerate for six to seven years.

It turns out that specialists have long considered community forestry to be more sustainable than alternatives (such as outside businesses managing a forest). This claim may seem hard to believe. Without getting too wonky, it's worth mentioning that an economist (Elinor Ostrom) won a Nobel Prize for Economic Sciences (the first woman to do so) in 2010 for her research on this issue. Go figure. Basically: those who live in a forest are better stewards of them. Community forestry is surprisingly widespread in the world and is considered one of the top means for limiting the devastation of climate change. Again, at the risk of lapsing into "academic" mode, Paul Hawken's book *Drawdown* contains supporting facts and statistics.

The Maroon see the greatest danger arising from a combination of greedy foreign corporations and corrupt officials that ought to be enforcing limits in areas outside of Maroon areas, which are called concessions. There, the deforestation was described by them, and by a veteran conservation worker in the region, as "total."

The 2020 COVID-19 pandemic makes the threat of encroaching mining worse

In Paramaribo, the veteran conservation worker just mentioned in the previous section showed me truly disturbing aerial photos: the comment above—that foreign interests and corrupt locals are destroying vast areas of jungle—was substantiated. Vast swaths of river to the east, near the French Guyanese border, were visibly filled with runoff from mining operations. This runoff is the worst damage—worse than logging, because the pollution contains toxins used in the process of separating and collecting gold.

The COVID-19 pandemic of 2020 had an impact on Suriname and other countries with rainforests, but not the impact you might expect. Ma' Bele points out that the Maroon villages were not so reliant on tourism for basic subsistence needs, plus they were isolated enough to avoid becoming infected with COVID-19. However, as gold prices skyrocketed (due to the world's rich sheltering their assets in this perceived safe store of value), this incentivized massive growth in illegal mining plus attendant poaching for food in what was left of many of the world's tropical rainforests. Elsewhere in the Guyanas and Amazon, this was a problem even before the pandemic, but the pandemic made it far worse.

The image at the end of this section was taken in early 2020 over Suriname, not far from the border of a protected area in French Guyana (which, because it is a part of France, is a European Union national park). The yellow coloration of the river is from mining site runoff. The location of the mines is visible on the right.

When I asked about wider environmental disruptions, Ma' Bele confirms that a changing climate has been observed, with floods being more rapid and floodwaters higher than what was previously experienced. And what will happen when the companies are done exploiting concessions elsewhere, I asked? Won't they approach the Maroon lands, onto what the Maroons call the plantations—where they plant, on a rotating basis, within the intact forest? "They might," Ma' Bele answered. "But that will be very bad. There will be a fight if that happens."

10.7. A river in Suriname appears yellow—when viewed in color—due to pollution from mining runoff. (Image courtesy of Katia Delvoye.)

It is enough to be Ma' Bele

I asked Ma' Bele whether he would want any role as a leader, since he's clearly respected and popular, relates well with seemingly everyone, and has an understanding of the outside world as well as an obvious love for his home community. "No," he answers, "though they asked me to be captain [their term for the equivalent of mayor], and I said no." It seems enough, I noted, that everyone considers Ma' Bele as effectively the uncle of the village. This includes the kids walking by every morning on their way to school and those who sit (on a rotating basis, determined by their teachers) at his laptop computers every evening, learning computer skills and geography.

I asked Ma' Bele if this is so—is it enough to be everyone's uncle? "Yes," he said with a smile. And he quickly confirmed and clarified two things: "Ma" means uncle (a good, if completely unintended, guess on my part), but his nickname "Bele" is not a variation of "Billy" (contrary to what I had intentionally tried to guess) but rather "belly"—a name he received in childhood thanks to a having a temporarily protruding waistline. To sum up, his name means Uncle Belly. He shared a picture (reproduced at the end of this section) to lend credibility to his story.

10.8. Ma' Bele in a boat, near the village of Jaw Jaw, Suriname. (Image by Adam J. Sulkowski.)

10.9. Ma' Bele (bottom left) as a child, with his family. (Image courtesy of Ma' Bele.)

Any regrets?

Ma' Bele reacted: "Regrets? None. I learn from all of my mistakes."

"You mentioned mistakes—so, what was your biggest one?" I asked.

Ma' Bele looked away and contemplated this question and his response for what seemed—even by his deliberate, meditative standards—a very long time. After some reflection, he stated softly and succinctly: "Not coming back to Jaw Jaw sooner."

Takeaway lessons that could help you in other situations in life and business

(1) A sense of home and belonging can be a powerful force.

(2) Achieving one life goal can mean profound sacrifices in terms of other life goals.

(3) Watch, ask questions, and listen to potential and current customers.

(4) Be ready to abandon one idea and switch to another if evidence clearly supports that decision.

(5) Local, community-based, traditional governance among people with a multigenerational interest at stake may make for better decisions regarding the long-term management of natural resources.

Chapter 11

Outer Space and Inner Space: Astrophysicist to Heart Hacker and MindMics

O NE FACTOR I USED when deciding whether to retell a story in this book was whether the geographic location will somehow interest you, the reader. I have included stories from geographic locations that may be unfamiliar to the reader. We conclude, in this chapter, with a story that starts at the ultimate extreme in terms of distance—in outer space, with the most distant objects in the universe: supermassive black holes. The story concludes at the opposite extreme: inner space—or, more precisely, a startup that makes use of the space between our ears to collect precise health and medical data.

Other factors I used for deciding which stories to retell were whether there was adversity and change involved. This last chapter features a founder and story that highlight both of those themes. First, the main character arrived in the US with a single suitcase. Second, the story illustrates navigating radical change: switching from studying astrophysics to starting a health technology company.

Anna's first data science career: using galaxies as a lens to observe black holes

As an astrophysicist, Anna Barnacka participated in projects that built and operated networks of huge Cherenkov telescopes in remote places like Namibia or mountains in Arizona. The telescopes capture gamma rays that are produced by actively feeding supermassive black holes. In addition, her pioneering work in the field of gravitational lensing earned her a NASA Einstein Fellowship at Harvard and a Copernicus Award.

Gravitational lensing sounds—and is—complicated. But a very rough and oversimplified analogy helps to get an idea of what skills are involved. Simple glass lenses—like those in a magnifying glass or binoculars or telescope—change how light rays (electromagnetic radiation) are received by our eyes, allowing us to see objects that are very small or very far away. Similarly, distant galaxies function like a glass lens in that they bend space-time, changing the way that electromagnetic radiation reaches us on Earth (more specifically, the magnification and the timing at which it arrives).

So, to fully articulate the analogy: imagine using a telescope (with glass lenses) to observe the moon. Now imagine replacing the moon with an object located billions of light-years away—specifically, active supermassive black holes—and imagine replacing the telescope with a galaxy located somewhere between the object (the black hole) and you, functioning as a lens.

To understand Anna's contribution to the field of gravitational lensing, it is important to note that supermassive black holes feast on stars and that black holes are messy eaters. When they pull stars into themselves, they spit out a lot of gamma rays. One challenge in monitoring these gamma rays from across the universe to learn about black holes is the insufficient resolution of gamma-ray telescopes. This is where gravitational lensing comes in handy. But to use it, people like Anna needed to figure out how to handle large data streams from telescopes, modeling, and signal processing. As we'll see, Anna's skillsets as an astrophysicist, including core activities of a data scientist like collecting data and then "separating the signal from the noise," led her to the next phase of her life.

Again, to be sure, what's described in this section is a crude and simplified "bumper sticker version" of Anna's early career. But it is enough for us to understand how skills honed in one career can be used in another context.

11.1. Dr. Anna Barnacka—an astrophysicist and the founder and CEO of the company MindMics—with a Cherenkov array telescope, in Namibia. (Image courtesy of Dr. Anna Barnacka.)

Act 2 of Anna's career: MindMics is conceived

Along the way, while earning two PhDs and working everywhere from Namibia to Warsaw to the American Southwest to Paris and to Harvard, Anna studied and practiced several disciplines to understand and tame stress. These included mindfulness meditation, martial arts, and the use of biofeedback. Incredibly, she realized, most of the means we have for gathering data on our bodily functions (like standard blood pressure cuffs) are actually two centuries old. Anna further realized that new wearable tech gizmos you have likely heard about or use (watches, earbuds, chest straps, etc.) are actually neither precise nor reliable enough for medical purposes.

As a data scientist—someone who had advanced our ability to gather data and then to make use of it—Anna turned her attention to where on the human body there could be an as-of-yet not fully utilized source of accurate, precise, and reliable data. Of all the options, she realized that the ear canals would be the best place to detect signals from blood flow. Anna adjusted earbuds so that they functioned like high-precision detectors. Convinced that her resulting earbuds and algorithm could help others reach their potential through optimized monitoring of medical data, Anna imagined a company called MindMics to bring her invention to the market of people wanting—or needing—cheaper and easier access to reliable information about their health.

11.2. Dr. Anna Barnacka—an astrophysicist and the founder and CEO of the company MindMics—with an early prototype demonstrating the collection of medical data via ear canals. (Image courtesy of Dr. Anna Barnacka.)

Act 3: business and legal acumen, plus relationships, lead to a path to scaling

In no particular order, here are highlights of Anna's path as a founder and CEO that, in the course of me retelling her story, audiences have identified as particularly inspiring and valuable.

(1) Enjoy your hobbies, be aware of whom you're meeting while pursuing them, and be mindful and careful in sharing your ideas

and goals. For example, Anna enjoys classical music. In the course of attending events in support of the Boston Philharmonic Orchestra, she came to know someone who became an adviser, early investor, member of the board, and friend who introduced her to other individuals who could support the founding and growth and success of MindMics.

(2) The generalizable advice of "being ready to pivot" is illustrated in the first years of Anna's journey. While she anticipated pursuing a consumer market approach, Anna and her team explored engaging with different markets. For example, world-renowned cardiologists immediately appreciated the unique value of Anna's breakthrough wearable tech: that it has the potential to change lives by providing unprecedented medical-grade precision, sometimes even more than what the state-of-the-art existing technology provides. The unprecedented insights from the data led Anna's team to explore a fit with the healthcare, insurance, and biopharmaceutical industries. Anna explained: "Regardless of which market and partners we engage[d] first, we knew we had to gather data and refine the earbuds, platform, and algorithms—it's important to strike a balance between strengthening the core of the value that we can offer, even as we remain open to considering options of when and how to deploy our technology."

(3) Anna drafted her first provisional patent herself. Several patents followed. Some are surprised that someone could teach themselves the steps to set up and run a company and even handle legal issues. This aspect of the story tends to inspire others to question the limitations that they may have set for themselves or, put another way, to wonder how much more they might be able to accomplish with the right mix of curiosity, a learner's mentality, discipline, and grit.

(4) On a similar note, another theme related to intellectual property, law, and strategy is how to strike a balance between openness, collaboration, and sharing (to attract investments and talent) while making sure that no one—including companies with vast resources—can copy you. One might assume that, to avoid being copied, anyone in Anna's position would be hyper-secretive. Yet information-sharing is necessary to build and run a company.

One reason Anna feels confident that no one will replicate MindMics's product, in addition to patenting her innovations, is that there are multiple other hurdles to surmount besides adjusting earbud components. MindMics is actually a platform. The full recipes for all three parts of the MindMics platform include (A) the hardware (the earbuds), (B) the data systems and algorithms (the cloud-based calculations to turn data into useful information), and (C) the interface for instantaneously seeing your vital signs (either on your cell phone or else on a website). Pictured at the end of this section is Anna at Scripps Research (a nonprofit medical research facility), which is one of the locations where this novel core technology is being tested in conjunction with state-of-the-art medical technologies.

The lesson that can be adopted for other situations is this: a defensible position is one that consists of several features, each of which is a challenge to create or duplicate. Designing anything— a product, a company, a charitable organization, or even your personal brand or value proposition—should similarly take into account whether there are several components or characteristics that are hard to duplicate or imitate. If this is the case, a legal "moat' like patent protection is still nice insurance—and one that many early-stage investors want to see—but not the only and indispensable source of protection from imitation.

To further substantiate this point, consider Tesla. Some of its technology is not completely novel, and Elon Musk decided to take an open-source approach to innovations—inviting the rest of the automotive industry to catch up technologically. This might be partially explained by wanting more entities lobbying for, and building, key infrastructure and contributing to refinements and economies of scale in some contexts. But it is also further evidence that there can be several aspects to a product, service, or organization that make it difficult to imitate or duplicate.

In response to this observation, Anna added that another key success factor is execution. In her words: "To build a complex system, you need to have someone who can build interdisciplinary teams, communicate in everyone's language, and motivate and drive the innovation forward no matter the obstacles, stresses, pandemics, competition, lack of funds, and all the other possible things that can go wrong. The leader has to wake up every morning and help the team create value even when the sky is falling."

(5) Diversity and inclusion are hot topics. A quick perusal of the MindMics website reveals a surprising variety of people working with Anna's company—which now employs or otherwise engages the expertise of dozens of talented individuals. The diversity of people on Anna's teams is not a result of recent woke-ness, although Anna is acutely aware of biases, having lived the experience of a recent immigrant to the United States and having succeeded in two male-dominated arenas: astrophysics and now a technology startup ecosystem. Instead, Anna asserted that, at least in her case, her focus on finding the best talent resulted in a remarkably diverse team.

11.3. Dr. Anna Barnacka—an astrophysicist and the founder and CEO of the company MindMics—at Scripps Research in San Diego, California, where MindMics technology is tested. (Image courtesy of Dr. Anna Barnacka.)

Takeaway lessons that could help you in other situations in life and business

(1) Ask how skills that you developed in one field can be used to solve another problem.

(2) As illustrated in other stories in this book, experiment with solving a problem that you have.

(3) In solving any problem, start with first principles. Use the scientific method for both innovation and running your operation: start with a guess (a hypothesis) about how things work. Test it. If it fails, revise your understanding about how things work (your theory) and come up with the next hypothesis to test.

(4) Be aware of whom you're meeting while enjoying your hobbies, as these acquaintances and friends and colleagues may enjoy providing critical help as you build your venture.

(5) As illustrated in other stories in this book, have passion and believe in your mission, but keep an open mind to big changes, including who will be your first clients and how your service will be used.

(6) Question what must be outsourced, what must be purchased, and your own limits of what you can and cannot do yourself. With a mix of curiosity, a learner's mentality, discipline, and grit, you may be able to accomplish more than you thought possible. As you build a team and acquire resources, you may then hire others to perform functions that you previously learned how to do.

(7) When it comes to your creative ideas, law, and planning your strategy, consider carefully a balance between openness, collaboration, and sharing. Some people err on the side of secrecy to avoid having ideas stolen or their business copied. Others realize that some information must be shared to attract investments and talent.

(8) A defensible position consists of several features, each of which is a challenge to create or duplicate. Then, a remaining critical success factor is execution, which requires communicating in diverse styles to motivate and coordinate multidisciplinary teams.

(9) An open and thorough search for the best talent can result in remarkably diverse teams (though, as noted above, an additional factor leading to this result may be if the person doing the recruiting is someone who is from a historically underrepresented demographic in her professional fields).

Conclusion

Takeaway Lessons in Fortune Cookie Form

THERE ARE DOUBTLESSLY many more stories in the world like the ones featured in this book or stories that are about to transpire. It may be yours, and I hope to hear it. Good luck making your story worthy of retelling!

Friends and colleagues have encouraged me to offer you, the reader, a final chapter that attempts to distill the takeaways of each chapter into a final "roadmap" for your own adventures in life. I've tweaked the suggestion to not only include a summation of ideas to keep in mind as an entrepreneur but also as a traveler. In fact, the following takeaways have been generalized enough to possibly apply to *any* situation.

Before you start

- Be honest with yourself about what you do not know. Embrace your ignorance. Get *excited* about your ignorance—and about asking the basic beginner's questions to fill gaps in what you know.

- There may be pieces of a puzzle around you for doing something constructive, fun, and possibly lucrative that you (and others) just haven't yet appreciated.

- Absorb information from a variety of sources. Keep an open mind.

- Start with your passion and mission—what you enjoy and find meaningful as serving a deeper purpose—and build your activities around them.

- Identify pain points, needs, or aspirations. In some cases, an inspiration for a new activity could be the pains or needs of others. In other cases, one's own needs are an inspiration for a new venture.

- Ask what skills you have developed and what your sense of a fulfilling mission involves, and test activities that are consistent with that personally meaningful, constructive purpose.

- Investigate what flexibility might exist within the laws of your location to do more with the same permit—or to possibly even get a permit to do what seems to be barred.

Seeing opportunities

- Have a balance of holistic thinking and laser-focused discipline on developing a core idea that could address a need.

- Be open to seeing opportunities that others may have missed— including those resulting from monstrous legacies, oversight, or perverse systems.

- Systems with shortcomings may present more than one opportunity to affect positive change—it is possible to have an impact through siting, methods, and employment.

- Be open to the possibility that there are other people who are eager to help or to partner to find solutions, improve approaches, and achieve better outcomes.

- People from different disciplines, from different realities, and with different lenses can see solutions to wicked problems that might elude a team of specialists in one discipline.

- Be ready to question ideological stances and boundaries.

- Some opportunities look doubtful at first, until more information is gathered.

- Step back, see the big picture, and connect the dots: there may be connections and relationships—between people, supply and demand, leading indicators, etc.—that others have failed to see.

Starting-up and finding resources

- Start. Nurture a predisposition toward action—ideally, a small, controlled risk to test an idea—rather than either over-planning or "betting everything all at once."

- Telling others about constructive ambitions can result in a surprising amount of support.

- A lack of resources can sometimes force experimentation, methods, discoveries, and results that are better than a context with an abundance of resources.

- Put off costs (especially when startup capital and credit are unavailable) and defer cash outflows and take cash upfront for whatever can be sold, rented out, or sublet.

- Find "waste" to reuse: idle or unused resources or those that are about to be discarded.

- Ask what you can do yourself or with volunteers (at first) before later hiring others to help.

Early activities

- Start with—and maintain—a core activity related to something you love but be willing to embrace "the drunkard's walk" or "pivoting"—adjusting to fresh information and opportunities and even changing the goal or strategy.

- Some solutions may not fit the textbook version of the ideal way of doing something; within reason, be open to putting trust in close friends and family and data and your instincts.

- Be open to see shortcomings—with the right adjustments—as opportunities to differentiate and find value.

Growing teams

- Do not underestimate people—especially the outliers and even those who are written off.

- By listening and showing respect, you may unlock undiscovered potential.

- As you engage in activities of any kind, remain open to starting and building relationships with people that will be happy to help your idea succeed.

- Hire for personality traits, not teachable skills.

- Be ready (both emotionally and in terms of recruitment activity) to let go people that damage morale and culture.

- Attract talent by sharing your vision and giving people the chance to exercise creativity, take ownership, and see the chance to create something exciting and new.

Dealing with setbacks

- Take stock of what you still have—you may be underappreciating the key assets in all of these stories: the goodwill, energy, ideas, and support of other people.

- A setback could lead to something positive, possibly even discovering one's mission in life or even finding a pioneering way of doing something.

- Focus on what can be done rather than limitations.

Marketing

- Delighted customers—and their word-of-mouth recommendations—are the best marketing and can be a lifeline in bad times.

- Supporting community initiatives is another invaluable form of marketing.

- Do not underestimate the number or the commitment of people that may value and support what you do, even in a place that outsiders may overgeneralize as being unsupportive or even hostile.

- Do not become overly reliant on one source of clients.

Trust, law, and relationships

- When contracts and rule of law are unreliable, reputation and relationships serve similar functions and become even more valuable in hard times. Yet there is a dichotomy to this observation. Don't ignore negotiating contracts, even with trusted partners. There is immense value in discussing—proactively—the needs of both sides, how both sides could fail, the consequences of failure, and how failures can be limited or remedied. This process of getting to know the interests and plans of both sides and establishing contingencies for the future is part of both a comprehensive approach to contracts and to building an understanding such that they never have to be enforced.

- A strong optimistic brand can be a key factor to success—to the point that sworn enemies on opposite sides of a long and deadly conflict (sometimes) may respect your organization and allow you to flourish and succeed.

- Consider more transparency, since ideas about how to improve processes and outcomes have come from an array of stakeholders inside and outside an organization.

Refining and developing and growing

- Consider soft openings and repeated iterations to test and improve your service.

- Put yourself in the customers' place, watch and listen to them, respect them, and keep a service-oriented and positively responsive mindset.

- Continuous and playful trial and error can, in reality, sometimes lead to breakthroughs in areas where theories have to date failed to provide a clear path toward solutions.

- Be ready to abandon an idea and switch to another if evidence clearly supports that decision.

- Build upon whatever makes you or your service unique.

- Put your heart into what you do. It can differentiate your service.

As your activities mature

- Magnifying your impact and leaving a sustainable legacy requires, at some point, delegating authority and trusting others.

- Avoid having indispensable employees—this may include people near the top of the organization. Instead, develop systems early and be ready to let go and replace people that negatively impact culture.

- Carving out a portion of time for one's own health and time with family—whether we call this work–life balance or work–life harmony—is recommended as essential for maintaining peace of mind and happiness.

- Achieving one life goal can mean profound sacrifices in terms of other life goals.

- Share and be proud of your work but remain teachable and open to input.

With regard to sustainability

- Re-localization of supply chains can result in healthier food options as well as jobs and local wealth creation.

- Restoring local pride in traditions can be constructive and the basis of a business; a sense of home and belonging can be powerful needs or desires.

- Local, community-based, traditional governance among people with a multigenerational interest at stake may make for better decisions regarding the long-term management of natural resources.

- Waste in one context can be a valuable asset in another context.

- Legacies and more recent history may have resulted in perverse realities, including situations where nutrient-poor imported food is more popular than locally-sourced healthy food. These flawed systems may actually present opportunities.

- In the face of massive problems, a constructive outlook and mindset can be maintained by focusing on whatever small steps can be taken in one's own realm of influence.

- Regenerative enterprises—organizations that generate more positive side effects than negative side effects—are possible.

- Innovation and profound changes can start from simple fundamentals like planting trees.

- A lack of resources and a commitment to finding net-zero emissions solutions can result in more resourcefulness and creativity and other valuable innovations.

Finally

- There is no substitute for a relentless work ethic, a sustained, regular, and disciplined effort, attention to detail, high standards, and being willing to sacrifice to put in the time needed to build and improve and deliver your service.

- Always be looking for the next opportunity to grow and improve, but be self-aware enough to know "when enough is enough" to avoid burn-out or overextension.

- Regardless of whether you can protect an innovation through patents, being known for continuous innovation and improvement is a better means of keeping clients.

- Stay loyal, even when times are bad—relationships within a business and with people outside your business continuously surface as indispensable, especially in extreme environments.

Afterword

Additional Travel Tips and Further Content

THERE WERE A FEW details that I cut from the chapters above. Some were facts related to authentic first impressions when arriving in a new place. Others were anecdotes. I removed them from the chapters because some readers may think that they perpetuate hurtful stereotypes of some countries. These items are included in this section (with the name of the country removed) because they are things that happen in a lot of countries, and there may be some value for you, the reader, in knowing about them.

The wealth gap

It may sound cliché, but some first impressions are truly unforgettable. For example: arriving in a new place on a cold night and seeing children sleeping side by side without blankets on sheets of cardboard in unlit streets with no parents in sight. My memory of seeing this is worth sharing because it does make a deep and lasting impact on a first-time visitor (or even a veteran traveler who has spent time in slums, refugee camps, etc.). And it helps to emphasize major themes of the stories in this book. Namely, that the main characters do not become immobilized in the face of all that is wrong but rather focus their attention on the potential of what could be and focus their efforts on creating a better future. The images of young kids asleep on cardboard on the street at night or picking through trash in the day also make it all the more jarring to come across the occasional obvious traces of the (sometimes opulent) European colonial past in some architecture, accommodations, and food and drink options offered to foreign visitors. When someone (either local or from somewhere else) invites you into such a fancy place for a meal, it can lead to some conflicting emotions. On the one hand, it feels wrong to consume a good meal (some of them unique and tasty) when you've just passed people in need. On the other, to paraphrase what Anthony Bourdain said about a similar question related to vegetarianism, do we want to seem to be an ungrateful guest and possibly seem disrespectful of a culture or tradition of hospitality if someone wants to be a generous host and invites us to share a meal?

It can be troubling to see the extent and the obviousness of the gap between haves and have-nots in some places. But here's something that needs to be pointed out before we get judgmental: massive wealth gaps, poverty, food insecurity, and homelessness exist in a lot of places, including the United States. Where I live and work in the Boston area, it's just easier for us to keep it out of sight and out of mind and pretend it's not there. Less so else-where. I'm still not sure which is better.

To come back to my main point in writing this section (and a motivation for writing this book): the world has problems. You could go crazy dwelling on every injustice and inequity (whether it's in our face or tidily kept out of sight). Instead, the heroes at the center of the stories in this book are able to look past dark realities and build something better for other people (and themselves).

Warning: be careful of people, but also be aware that many people tend to be nicer than we expect

A first-time visitor to many places on Earth experiences warnings. There are cities where everyone warns you, as a visitor, to not walk alone at night (or sometimes even in broad daylight) for fear of being robbed (or worse). This warning was once repeated to me by a random fellow who happened to sit next to me at the end of a trip through a country. He showed me a crime report with some grim numbers and shared details of how some irresponsible visitors met their end. He claimed to work for GS4, the largest private employer in Africa, specializing in security for government officials and businesspeople. He seemed surprised that visitors and expats (including solo travelers of different gender identities) wandered the country we were in.

The reason I mention this warning is twofold. First, if the stories in this book inspire you to travel—locally or abroad—it's good, anytime and anywhere, to use some common sense. My advice is to always reach out to locals and other travelers and look for company, especially when traveling solo. Second, a recurring theme in these stories—whether it involves the entrepreneurs or my own luck—is that, if you need help, reach out and ask: people can be remarkably generous and kind, often when you most need it.

In other words, there's a dichotomy between being an entrepreneur like the people in this book and being on the road. You must prepare for the worst. But you must hope for the best and be open to the possibility that good things are about to happen, both because of planning (and sometimes luck) and very often because of a kind stranger you're about to meet.

For all the well-intentioned and well-founded warnings, I have heard many other travelers (of all genders, races, and nationalities) confirm something: everywhere (across cultures and regions), a big share of people are authentically kind—more of them, and more often than we have any right to reasonably expect. People help. They give tips. They share information. Some offer much more. It's instinctual. Sometimes they might expect something back. But usually, strangers help for no particular reason other than it feels good. Sometimes their sense of pride—"This is how we treat guests in our culture"—clearly overwhelms their potential initial instincts to transact and just get some money out of you. The corollary to this observation may be obvious: just as we're surprised and grateful when a stranger offers help, it may be wise to nurture a mindset and practice of being helpful and generous yourself—whether or not you believe that "what goes around comes around."

There are bad people who do bad things. It's good to be proactive and avoid situations where something bad can happen. But it is also good to ask for (and to give) help. A greater share of people are better than we might expect.

Respect and saying no to drama: one option if you are asked for a bribe

The following happens in a lot of places. A taxi I was in was stopped by some type of policeman in a camouflage uniform. I quickly understood that he was asking me for my Carte Jaune or Yellow Card. It's proof of vaccination against certain diseases. It's required to travel to and from some countries. I had checked earlier. The country we were in was definitely *not* one of them. So, I didn't have mine with me. I told him I was sure it wasn't needed. He assumed an air of authority and replied that I'd be charged a fine if I didn't pay him to help me.

The taxi driver was somber and serious, looking straight

ahead and avoiding eye contact. He seemed to have realized, long before I did—probably from the moment the policeman signaled for us to stop—that I'd be asked to pay a bribe. It was a new experience for me, and I remember wondering how far this armed fellow wanted to escalate his demand for a payment. Much like John Rexer in the chapter on Ilegal Mezcal, I honestly can't say from where the inspiration hit me to say the following words. I think our having passed various embassy compounds just minutes earlier may have triggered the following reply in what I hoped was comprehensible French: "Please, then, could you kindly take me to my embassy?"

The policeman changed his demeanor. "Oh, I was just trying to help. You can go." He waved and stepped back. As we drove on, the taxi driver burst out laughing. I think we both laughed and repeated the dialogue in celebration, as if a Jedi mind trick had just been successfully performed. Shaking his head, he asked if this was my standard reply. Well, it is now. While I've never (so far, knock on wood) paid a bribe, it may be safer in some situations to just make a donation, or a gift, or "cadeaux" as it's called in some places.

To emphasize one more time: similar problems can arise in a lot of places. Recent years have made it obvious that there are some police everywhere (including in the US) that are less than great. Plus, I don't want to diminish the reality that our race or gender or national origin can affect the outcome of these situations. Or that they can end very badly. Maybe one last reflection to share is that, as in any human interaction, it may help to try to act polite, calm, and confident (even if you're a bit worried on the inside), to not contradict or argue, and to show respect by actually asking for help.

Similarly, this is another, more general—and related— observation about the people in the stories in this book: they obviously experience emotions but generally seem to stay calm, friendly, and respectful of people around them, regardless of the situation. This seems to be a trait they all have in common: authentic respect for themselves, their teams, clients, and others (including strangers) and not having an attitude or instinct for drama or "a chip on their shoulder" (even if some have every right to be frustrated with reality and other people). My profound thanks to the individuals and teams described in this book's stories for the good examples they are setting.

One more time, good luck!

Here's hoping you found something valuable and interesting in the stories in this book. And I wish you good luck (again) in your adventures. If you have questions or know of similar stories that you think I should consider for a follow-up book, please do not hesitate to contact me directly—my contact information appears in the About the Author section toward the back of this book. In addition, to read or hear my most recent stories and conversations with people like the ones in this book, please visit www.extreme-entrepreneurship.com.

From the Publisher

Thank You from the Publisher

Van Rye Publishing, LLC ("VRP") sincerely thanks you for your interest in and purchase of this book.

VRP hopes you will please consider taking a moment to help other readers like you by leaving a rating or review of this book at your favorite online book retailer. Depending on the retailer, you can do so by flipping past the last page of your e-book (to the rating and review page) or by visiting the book's product page (and locating the button for leaving a rating or review).

Thank you!

Resources from the Publisher

Van Rye Publishing, LLC ("VRP") offers the following resources to readers and to writers.

For *readers* who enjoyed this book or found it useful, please consider receiving updates from VRP about new and discounted books like this one. You can do so by following VRP on Facebook (at www.facebook.com/vanryepub) or Twitter (at www.twitter.com/vanryepub).

For *writers* who enjoyed this book or found it useful, please consider having VRP edit, format, or fully publish your own book manuscript. You can find out more and submit your manuscript at VRP's website (at www.vanryepublishing.com).

Thank you again!

Acknowledgments

THIS IS—UNAVOIDABLY, given the nature of collecting these stories—an incomplete list, but I give huge thanks to the following individuals.

First, to those profiled in this book, for your time, inspiration, patience, and allowing me to share your stories (in order of appearance): Dr. Liliana Mayo, Aysha Raja, Cesar Gaio and Bob Howarth, John Rexer, Camille Dazyk and Iry Raïssa Alaoy and Aurelie Buffo and Suzanne Jaouen and Ken Lee Randrianarisoa, Paolo Lugari, Lieutenant Colonel Faye Cuevas and Lydia Wanjiku Kibandi, Rodolfo Baster, Karim El-Gamal and Michael Kasseris, Ma' Bele, and Dr. Anna Barnacka.

For your contribution of supporting commentary, perspectives, "reality checks," editing, input, introductions, and support of all kinds (in order of chapter-specific expertise): Rafay Ahmad Alam, Rebecca Ellen Engel, Virgilio Guterres, Luis Soares, Nico Livache, Eric Klose, Professor Mónica Ramos Mejía of Pontificia Universidad Javeriana in Bogotá, Colombia, Jason Kleinerman, Katya Delvoye, Associate Professor Mystica Alexander of Bentley University, Professor D. Steven White of the University of Massachusetts Dartmouth, and Professor George Siedel of the University of Michigan, plus all those involved in the professional editing, publishing, and promotion of this book, including Van Rye Publishing.

An earlier iteration of the story described in chapter eight won the International Case Writing Award at the 2016 annual conference of the Academy of Legal Studies in Business and was published in the Journal of Legal Studies Education as *Rodolfo's Casa Caribe in Cuba: Business, Ethical & Legal Challenges of Investing in a Start-Up in Havana* (Vol. 34, No. 1, Pages 127–162). An earlier iteration of the content collected and described in chapter nine won an award at the 2017 annual meeting of the United States Association for Small Business and Entrepreneurship and appeared in the proceedings of the conference as a submission coauthored with the following colleagues at Babson College: Associate Professor Angela Randolph, Associate Professor Benjamin Luippold, and Assistant Professor Jennifer Bailey. Thanks also to my colleague Professor Bob Turner, also of Babson College, for introducing me to the protagonists of that story in the fall of 2015.

Thanks to family, friends, and strangers—those who asked not to be named or whose name I never knew—that have been kinder and more supportive than anyone had any right to expect.

Last but not least, thanks to students—the "beta testers"—who've heard or read or discussed these stories or engaged in Q & A with people profiled in this book.

This book is dedicated to all of you—especially the good people profiled in it—in the hope that your stories continue inspiring the next set of stories worth telling.

About the Author

A DAM J. SULKOWSKI is an associate professor of law and sustainability at Babson College, ranked as the #1 school for entrepreneurs for decades, according to *US News & World Report* and other authorities. As a professor since 2005, he has earned tenure twice (at UMass Dartmouth and again at Babson), has won more than a dozen teaching and research awards, has been published over fifty times (including over three dozen times in academic journals), and was a Fulbright Scholar (in 2014–15). Before beginning his teaching career, Professor Sulkowski received a BA from the College of William & Mary and an MBA and JD from Boston College. He also ran a business and worked as an attorney at firms, at businesses, and on behalf of environmental causes.

Professor Sulkowski grew up in the greater Boston area as the multilingual first child of two immigrant scientists who survived war and communism. Stories passed on from his grandmother about the improbable survival of his relatives made him intrigued by other times and places and helped inspire his interest in travel—"the further from home, the better," he says. Professor Sulkowski has now visited over 120 countries, including as a visiting faculty member of the Warsaw University of Life Sciences. Wherever he is, he feels most at home in conversations, whether in classrooms or (especially) on the road with people solving big problems in hard times and tough places. He has a passion for turning those conversations into stories that entertain, educate, and inspire others.

You can follow or contact Professor Sulkowski on Twitter (www.twitter.com/adam_sulkowski), on LinkedIn (www.linkedin .com/in/adamsulkowski), or via email (asulkowski@babson.edu).